C0 ALL637

QA
76.9
.D6
B76
1984

GUIDE

TO EFFECTIVE

SOFTWARE

TECHNICAL

WRITING

CHRISTINE BROWNING

PRENTICE-HALL, INC., *Englewood Cliffs, New Jersey 07632*

GOSHEN COLLEGE LIBRARY
GOSHEN, INDIANA

Library of Congress Cataloging in Publication Data

Browning, Christine.
  Guide to effective software technical writing.

  Includes index.
  1. Electronic data processing documentation.
2. Technical writing. I. Title.
QA76.9.D6B76 1984   808'.066001   84-6788
ISBN 0-13-369463-1
ISBN 0-13-369455-0 (pbk.)

Editorial/production supervision and interior design: **Karen Skrable**
Cover design: **Jeannette Jacobs**
Manufacturing buyer: **Gordon Osbourne**

© 1984 by **Prentice-Hall, Inc.**, Englewood Cliffs, New Jersey 07632

*All rights reserved. No part of this book may be
reproduced, in any form or by any means,
without permission in writing from the publisher.*

Printed in the United States of America

10 9 8 7 6 5 4 3 2 1

ISBN 0-13-369463-1
ISBN 0-13-369455-0 {PBK} 01

PRENTICE-HALL INTERNATIONAL, INC., *London*
PRENTICE-HALL OF AUSTRALIA PTY. LIMITED, *Sydney*
EDITORA PRENTICE-HALL DO BRASIL, LTDA., *Rio de Janeiro*
PRENTICE-HALL CANADA INC., *Toronto*
PRENTICE-HALL OF INDIA PRIVATE LIMITED, *New Delhi*
PRENTICE-HALL OF JAPAN, INC., *Tokyo*
PRENTICE-HALL OF SOUTHEAST ASIA PTE. LTD., *Singapore*
WHITEHALL BOOKS LIMITED, *Wellington, New Zealand*

CONTENTS

PREFACE

Computers are one of our most dynamic and fastest-growing modern industries. But how can you become a part of and even play a key role in this environment without being a computer programmer, mathematician, or engineer?

One part of the computer industry that is open to people with a variety of backgrounds is documentation.

Manufacturers cannot sell computers, software (programs), or accessories unless they provide manuals that tell the customers how to use these products.

The manuals are *not* written by the computer designers and programmers. Even if these technical experts had the time, they would not necessarily have the literary expertise to do the job.

If you

have good communication skills,

believe you can develop a sound writing craft,

are interested in computers,

are willing to learn about the software, and

enjoy helping people to learn,

consider software technical writing, one of the most profitable and rewarding careers in the computer industry.

This book describes how to write good software manuals. It does not assume a strong background in computer technology, but it does assume a strong desire to learn. Writing any type of software manual requires an understanding of the subject and an ability to communicate effectively with the software expert who supplies the information.

- If you are a software technical writer already, this book can help you improve your skills.
- If you are a technical writer who is planning to move into the field of software technical writing, this book can teach you mechanics that minimize the writing effort.
- If you are interested in exploring the possibility of becoming a software technical writer, this book will show you the basic principles of manual writing. Many of these principles also apply to writing computer-related material, such as brochures, promotional literature, and magazine articles.

Chapter 1 introduces software manual writing. It describes why manuals are important, explains their functions, and gives the criteria for writing them.

Chapter 2 describes how to organize the text, establish the readership, and plan the writing task.

Chapter 3 gives a step-by-step approach to writing a software reference manual.

Chapter 4 gives a step-by-step approach to writing a software user manual.

Chapter 5 discusses techniques for structuring a manual to increase its usability.

Chapter 6 presents a style guide. It explains how to ensure readability and avoid common mistakes that detract from the usability of a manual.

Chapter 7 describes the front matter. This includes the revision record, preface, table of contents, and syntax conventions.

Chapter 8 describes the back matter. This includes the appendixes, glossary, and index.

Chapter 9 is an example to test your comprehension.

The glossary provides definitions of computer industry terminology.

Skilled technical writers can play a key role as intermediaries between users and technical experts. The computer will never fulfill its potential unless people can learn to appreciate it and use it effectively. The challenge of providing the required teaching material is open to anyone who finds it exciting and worthwhile.

ACKNOWLEDGMENT

Computer systems, with their text-editing facilities, disk and tape units, and high-speed printers, simplify the writer's task. For making their special equipment available to me, I am deeply grateful to Tandem Computers Incorporated, Cupertino, CA.

Christine Browning

1/WHAT IS A SOFTWARE MANUAL?

Organizations associated with the computer industry market a variety of software products. Each of these products requires at least one manual that describes its design and operation.

Airlines, for example, use software products that maintain their flight reservation data. Suppose you are taking a trip.

The reservation agent books your flight

by using a computer terminal

↓

to access computer software

↓

designed and coded by analysts and programmers

↓

who use software manuals

↓

to do their jobs.

What happens if the manuals are not complete and accurate?

The analysts and programmers make mistakes,

the computer software does not work the way it is supposed to,

the computer terminal delivers incorrect information, and you are booked on the wrong flight!

If this gives you some idea of how important software manuals are, consider the manuals that describe software for air traffic control. It is better for you to miss a flight than for the pilot to miss a runway.

WHO WRITES THE MANUALS?

Software manuals are written by specialized writers called software technical writers. These individuals have writing skills, a general knowledge of computer hardware, and a good knowledge of computer software. They take complicated subjects, organize them into logical pieces of information, and produce software manuals that serve as reference or learning tools.

The writers are often writing about new software or new software features with which they are not necessarily familiar. They are often writing the manuals at the same time the software is being developed. How can they do this? By seeking out information from the software designers and developers and by drawing on past experience—similar products, similar concepts.

Software technical writers fall into one of three categories:

1. The junior writer adds update material to existing software manuals, doing relatively little new or original writing.
2. The intermediate writer adds update material to existing software manuals and incorporates a certain amount of new and original writing.
3. The senior writer designs and writes new software manuals.

Each type of writer plays a critical role in the computer industry. Each has a responsibility to write clearly, concisely, accurately, and—always important—quickly.

The customer is eager to have the software, and the developer is eager to deliver it. But the software will not go anywhere without a manual that explains it.

WHAT DOES A SOFTWARE MANUAL LOOK LIKE?

A software manual has its own special format. Formats vary from company to company, but they generally look something like the one shown in Figure 1-1.

- The manual is divided into sections.
- The section carries a running head that identifies the subject matter.
- The section is numbered.
- The section title identifies a major area.
- The first-order paragraph head identifies a major topic within the area.
- The second-order paragraph head identifies a topic subordinate to the first-order paragraph head, and so forth.
- The manual is paginated by section. Pages can be added to one section without forcing other sections to be repaginated.

Breaking down information into these logical units serves several important purposes:

1. Information parallels the structure of the software product and helps readers to learn. A paragraph head *Control Statement Parameters* would probably be followed by subordinate paragraph heads for each of the parameters. Readers first learn that control statements have parameters, and then they find out exactly what those parameters are.
2. The material can be easily maintained. A software manual is usually updated rather than rewritten each time the product changes. The paragraph heads provide logical divisions for adding new or changing existing information. If the product is changed to include three new control statement parameters, the next writer already has a convenient place to put them.

Running Head

Third Order Paragraph Head

~~~~~~~~~~~~~~~~~~~~~~~~~~~~~~
~~~~~~~~~~~~~~~~~~~~~~~~~~~~~~
~~~~~~~~~~~~~~~~~~~~~~~~~~~~~~
~~~~~~~~~~~~~~~~~~~~~~~~~~~~~~

Third Order Paragraph Head

~~~~~~~~~~~~~~~~~~~~~~~~~~~~~~
~~~~~~~~~~~~~~~~~~~~~~~~~~~~~~
~~~~~~~~~~~~~~~~~~~~~~~~~~~~~~
~~~~~~~~~~~~~~~~~~~~~~~~~~~~~~

FOURTH ORDER PARAGRAPH HEAD. ~~~~~~~~~
~~~~~~~~~~~~~~~~~~~~~~~~~~~~~~
~~~~~~~~~~~~~~~~~~~~~~~~~~~~~~
~~~~~~~~~~~~~~~~~~~~~~~~~~~~~~
~~~~~~~~~~~~~~~~~~~~~~~~~~~~~~

FOURTH ORDER PARAGRAPH HEAD. ~~~~~~~~~~
~~~~~~~~~~~~~~~~~~~~~~~~~~~~~~
~~~~~~~~~~~~~~~~~~~~~~~~~~~~~~
~~~~~~~~~~~~~~~~~~~~~~~~~~~~~~
~~~~~~~~~~~~~~~~~~~~~~~~~~~~~~

FIRST ORDER PARAGRAPH HEAD

~~~~~~~~~~~~~~~~~~~~~~~~~~~~~~
~~~~~~~~~~~~~~~~~~~~~~~~~~~~~~
~~~~~~~~~~~~
~~~~~~~~~~~~
~~~~~~~~~~~~
~~~~~~~~~~~~
~~~~~~~~~~~~
~~~~~~~~~~~~
~~~~~~~~~~~~
~~~~~~~~~~~~

1-2

SECTION 1
SECTION TITLE

~~~~~~~~~~~~~~~~~~~~~~~~~~~~~~
~~~~~~~~~~~~~~~~~~~~~~~~~~~~~~
~~~~~~~~~~~~~~~~~~~~~~~~~~~~~~
~~~~~~~~~~~~~~~~~~~~~~~~~~~~~~
~~~~~~~~~~~~~~~~~~~~~~~~~~~~~~

FIRST ORDER PARAGRAPH HEAD

~~~~~~~~~~~~~~~~~~~~~~~~~~~~~~
~~~~~~~~~~~~~~~~~~~~~~~~~~~~~~
~~~~~~~~~~~~~~~~~~~~~~~~~~~~~~
~~~~~~~~~~~~~~~~~~~~~~~~~~~~~~

Second Order Paragraph Head

~~~~~~~~~~~~~~~~~~~~~~~~~~~~~~
~~~~~~~~~~~~~~~~~~~~~~~~~~~~~~
~~~~~~~~~~~~~~~~~~~~~~~~~~~~~~
~~~~~~~~~~~~~~~~~~~~~~~~~~~~~~

Second Order Paragraph Head

~~~~~~~~~~~~~~~~~~~~~~~~~~~~~~
~~~~~~~~~~~~~~~~~~~~~~~~~~~~~~
~~~~~~~~~~~~~~~~~~~~~~~~~~~~~~
~~~~~~~~~~~~~~~~~~~~~~~~~~~~~~

Third Order Paragraph Head

~~~~~~~~~~~~~~~~~~~~~~~~~~~~~~
~~~~~~~~~~~~~~~~~~~~~~~~~~~~~~
~~~~~~~~~~~~~~~~~~~~~~~~~~~~~~
~~~~~~~~~~~~~~~~~~~~~~~~~~~~~~

1-1

FIGURE 1-1 Software Manual Format

3. Readers are alerted to subject matter and can skip over the familiar or concentrate on the unfamiliar. The paragraph head *Control Statement Parameters* and its subordinate information can be safely ignored by the reader who is not planning to use control statements.

The Appearance of the Manual Is Important

A good novel that consists of page after page of unbroken text holds the reader's interest. The novel has an exciting plot.

A good software manual that consists of page after page of unbroken text does not hold the reader's interest. The manual has no plot.

Good software manuals have text that is broken up in several ways:

- indented text
- indented text preceded by bullets, as shown here
- short paragraphs
- programming examples, often printed in a different type font
- tables
- numbered steps
- illustrations

Figure 1-2 shows the difference between unbroken and broken text. If you had your choice of learning information from one of these sample pages, which page would you select?

The Content of the Manual Is More Important

A manual must do more than look good. To be effective and reflect professionalism, a manual should meet the following criteria:

1. *Material is well organized.* The manual is organized to serve the reader, not to satisfy the writer. A manual is always rated by its usability rather than by its literary style.

The SCANNER and PROC routines perform polling and character processing operations. SCANNER polls all lines in the network and upon detection of an input character, performs a series of tests to determine the legality of the input character. In addition, SCANNER calls a special-purpose routine to set pointers to four core-resident buffers: Term Buffer, Verify Buffer; Format Buffer, and Data Buffer. Term Buffer reflects terminal status; Verify Buffer maintains current record processing parameters; Format Buffer holds the memory address where the format is stored; and Data Buffer holds the input characters until they comprise a full record and require transmission. The pointers are established when the first input character is moved into the Data Buffer.

After the last input character has been verified, SCANNER calls the PROC routine. PROC checks the input characters against the stored format, interprets the operation to be performed, and then transfers control to the appropriate processing routine.

When the polling cycle is complete control passes to the EXECUTIVE program. If an input/output operation is required, the EXECUTIVE calls the appropriate driver, sets the I/O request word to zero, and returns control to SCANNER to continue the polling operations.

Term Buffer

The Term Buffer, which is allocated in ring 5, is a 2-word area that reflects the status of the terminal. Bit positions in word 1 are set to provide specific information regarding terminal activity. Bit 0 is set for input/output, bit 1 for read, bit 2 for write, bit 3 for error recovery, and bit 5 for parity checking. The remaining positions are reserved for future expansion.

Word 2 is the address of the diagnostic library. This word points to the message that is displayed in case of error. If no error has occurred, word 2 is set to 77777 octal.

Verify Buffer

The Verify Buffer, which is allocated in ring 4, is a 3-word area that holds the current record processing parameters. Each bit position indicates an operating mode. Bit 1 is set for read, bit 2 for write, bit 3 for read/write, bit 4 for read/lock, and bit 5 for recover mode.

The SCANNER and PROC routines perform polling and character processing operations.

SCANNER performs the following functions:

- polls all lines in the network and upon detection of an input character, performs a series of tests to determine the legality of the input character

- calls a special-purpose routine to set pointers to four core-resident buffers:

  - Term Buffer reflects terminal status.

  - Verify Buffer maintains current record processing parameters.

  - Format buffer holds the memory address where the format is stored.

  - Data Buffer holds the input characters until they comprise a full record and require transmission.

The pointers are established when the first input character is moved into the Data Buffer. After the last input character has been verified, SCANNER calls the PROC routine.

PROC performs the following functions:

- checks the input characters against the stored format

- interprets the operation to be performed

- transfers control to the appropriate processing routine.

When the polling cycle is complete, control passes to the EXECUTIVE program. If an input/output operation is required, the EXECUTIVE performs the following:

- calls the appropriate driver

- sets the I/O request word to zero

- returns control to SCANNER to continue the polling operations.

FIGURE 1-2 Unbroken and Broken Text

2. *Text is straightforward.* These sentences are not straight-forward:

> There is one major program in the application: MONI-TOR.

> No zeros to the right of the decimal point are suppressed.

But these sentences are:

> MONITOR is the major program in the application.

> Zeros to the right of the decimal point are not sup-pressed.

3. *Text is clear and concise.* This sentence is not clear:

> If the list option is selected, the last scanned line of source text is listed.

But this sentence is:

> If you select the list option, the last line of source text scanned by the compiler is listed on the output device.

This sentence is probably clear:

> From the programmer's point of view, you should deter-mine what routines are needed, what arrangement the routines should be grouped in, and when it is necessary to consider making procedure calls.

But this sentence is clear and concise:

> Determine what routines are needed, how they should be grouped, and when procedure calls should be made.

4. *Text is precise.* Precise text is complete text, leaving noth-ing to the reader's imagination. The description of a square root routine, for example, would include operations for negative as well as positive numbers.

This sentence is not precise:

> The RESULT field should be larger than the X and Y fields.

But this sentence is:

> The RESULT field should be at least 4 character posi-tions larger than the X and Y fields to prevent trunca-tion of high-order digits.

5. *Text provides only one interpretation.* Each of these sentences provides two interpretations:

> The conversion routine may be called by the main program.

A key field may not be duplicated.

But each of these sentences provides only one interpretation:

The conversion routine can be called by the main program.

A key field must not be duplicated.

6. *Illustration and table callouts are consistent.* Callouts in a manual can appear in sentence form or in abbreviated form. These two callouts for Figure 9-1 illustrate callouts in sentence form:

The XYZ routine performs conversion as shown in Figure 9-1.

Figure 9-1 illustrates conversion performed by the XYZ routine.

Intermixing these two types of callouts throughout the manual adds variety but does not introduce inconsistency.

These five callouts for Figure 9-1 illustrate callouts in abbreviated form:

The XYZ routine performs conversion (see Figure 9-1).

The XYZ routine performs conversion. See Figure 9-1.

The XYZ routine performs conversion (Figure 9-1).

The XYZ routine performs conversion (refer to Figure 9-1).

The XYZ routine performs conversion. Refer to Figure 9-1.

Intermixing these five types of callouts throughout the manual introduces inconsistency.

Intermixing abbreviated callouts with sentence callouts guarantees inconsistency.

7. *Illustrations and tables are complete with explanatory comments included in the illustration or table, not scattered throughout surrounding text.* If an illustration or table appears on page 5, its important notes should not appear on page 4, page 6, or worse, a combination of the two.

8. *Illustrations and tables are meaningful.* Illustrations should clarify concepts, not add variety to the format of the page. Figure 1-3 contrasts a meaningless and a meaningful illustration.

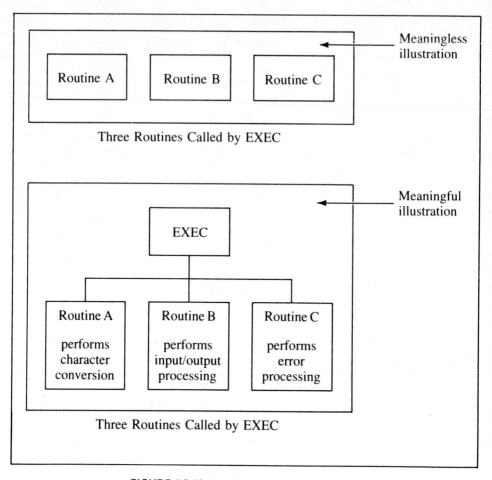

Meaningless
illustration

Three Routines Called by EXEC

Meaningful
illustration

Three Routines Called by EXEC

FIGURE 1-3 Keeping Illustrations Meaningful

Tables should serve as instant references, not complicated groupings that are difficult to decipher. Figure 1-4 contrasts a meaningless and a meaningful table.

9. *Illustrations and tables are uncluttered.* Illustrations should augment text, not add confusion. Figure 1-5 contrasts a cluttered and an uncluttered illustration.

Tables should include specific and exclude extraneous information. Figure 1-6 contrasts a cluttered and an uncluttered table.

10. *Writing style is consistent, especially when one writer is updating another writer's manual.* Readers can easily detect differences in writing style. They consciously or

Clause	Input Field	Output Field
Name		L
Conversion	L	L
Size	I	L
Padding		L*
Move	L*	L
Like	I	L
Exact	L	L +
Skip	L + *	I

blank	clause not allowed
L	legal
I	illegal
*	Size or Exact required
+	size = 30

Meaningless table ←

Clause	Can Be Used with an Input Field	Can Be Used with an Output Field
Conversion	X	X
Exact	X	X[1]
Like		X
Move	X[2]	X
Name		X
Padding		X[2]
Size		X
Skip	X[1][2]	

Note [1] The field must be 30 characters long.

Note [2] A Size or Exact clause is also required.

Meaningful table ←

FIGURE 1-4 Keeping Tables Meaningful

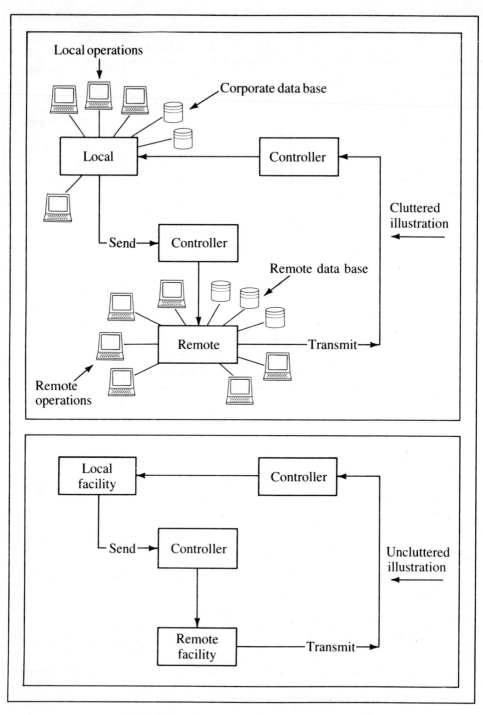

FIGURE 1-5 Keeping Illustrations Uncluttered

subconsciously realize the manual lacks quality. Figure 1-7 presents two paragraphs that were obviously written by two different writers.

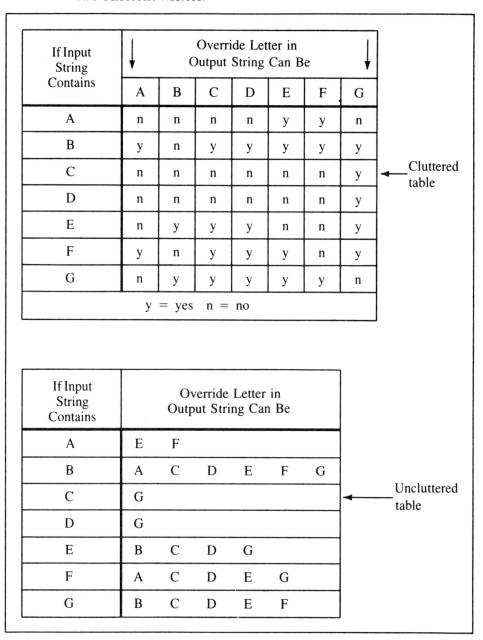

If Input String Contains	Override Letter in Output String Can Be						
	A	B	C	D	E	F	G
A	n	n	n	n	y	y	n
B	y	n	y	y	y	y	y
C	n	n	n	n	n	n	y
D	n	n	n	n	n	n	y
E	n	y	y	y	n	n	y
F	y	n	y	y	y	n	y
G	n	y	y	y	y	y	n
y = yes n = no							

← Cluttered table

If Input String Contains	Override Letter in Output String Can Be					
A	E	F				
B	A	C	D	E	F	G
C	G					
D	G					
E	B	C	D	G		
F	A	C	D	E	G	
G	B	C	D	E	F	

← Uncluttered table

FIGURE 1-6 Keeping Tables Uncluttered

Writer 1

Columns 1 through 5 are reserved for optional statement numbers. Statement numbers are not required, but if used, they cannot be duplicated within the program. Statement numbers need not appear in ascending numeric sequence. A maximum of 200 statement numbers can be used in one program. Statement number positioning is shown in Figure 9-3.

Writer 2

The directive portion of a statement can appear in columns 6-65. If a statement exceeds column 65, you can continue the statement in column 6 of the next line. When you continue a directive, you must include an asterisk (*) in column 1 of the continued line (see Figure 9-4).

> Writer 2 did not structure the first sentence to match the first sentence of Writer 1, even though the paragraphs were related.
>
> Writer 2 used a different convention for indicating column ranges.
>
> Writer 2 preferred to write in second person.
>
> Writer 2 used a different callout convention for illustrations.

FIGURE 1-7 Different Writing Styles

THE GOAL OF THE SOFTWARE MANUAL

The goal of any software manual is to be a complete, clear, and accurate description, presented in a manner suitable to the intended audience. This definition is just as complicated as it sounds.

> *Complete* implies thoroughness.
> *Clear* implies readability.
> *Accurate* implies authority.
> *Manner* implies organization.
> *Intended audience* implies recognition of reader level.

The good software manual includes every single one of these listed characteristics.

The software technical writer who produces that manual appears to face an enormous challenge.

THE GOAL OF THE SOFTWARE TECHNICAL WRITER

If a software manual is expected to meet the goal stated in the preceding paragraph, we can assume the goal of the software technical writer is to:

understand the subject to achieve thoroughness,

write well to achieve readability,

research the subject to achieve authority,

plan carefully to achieve organization, and

recognize the audience to achieve understandability.

This is not as complicated as it sounds. The secret is in the approach, and that is what this book is all about.

2/THE IMPORTANCE OF ORGANIZATION

Organization is the most important ingredient in a software manual. A poorly constructed sentence can be repaired by a literary editor; a technically inaccurate statement can be corrected by a technical editor; but a poorly organized manual is beyond help.

Organization is the arrangement of text to serve a specific purpose and a specific reader. The purpose of software text falls into one of two general categories; the reader of the text falls into one of several categories.

The organization of software reference text differs sharply from the organization of tutorial text.

Reference text is well organized when readers are able to locate specific information about the product and locate that information quickly.

Tutorial text is well organized when information is presented in an orderly sequence ranging from basic to complex. Readers can learn the operations and actually use the product while they are reading the text.

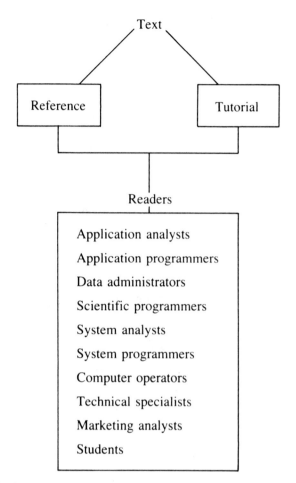

The levels of technical expertise among readers will always vary, but all readers can be regarded as specialists; they share with one another a common knowledge of the basic principles surrounding computer technology.

ORGANIZING THE TEXT

No two software products operate in exactly the same manner.

No two software technical writers write in exactly the same manner.

No two editors evaluate a software manual in exactly the same manner.

No two readers use a software manual in exactly the same manner.

No two publication departments function in exactly the same manner.

The software industry is in a constant state of change. Rigid standards that apply to all products on the market, suit all possible situations, and satisfy all the people all the time simply do not exist.

As a software technical writer, you can live with this problem by establishing some basic guidelines for organizing text. You can modify these guidelines as you move from one assignment to another in the industry.

Organizing Reference Text

Four principal rules can be applied to the organization of reference text.

1. *Define entities when they are first referenced.* For example: Define an entity the first time it appears in text and make the definition a major index entry.

2. *Centralize related entities.* For example: Describe a collection of related entities, such as programming statements, in one section for easy lookup.

3. *Arrange text in logical blocks of information.* For example: Discuss special programming subjects, such as character conversion, one time and in one place so they become standard points of reference.

4. *Include cross-references to related information.* For example: Direct the reader to the section describing a specific operation if that operation applies to the subject under discussion.

A beginning software technical writer was once assigned the task of writing a reference manual for an extremely complicated software product. The final draft consisted of only two sections:

• Section 1 introduced the product. The section totaled 3 pages.

- Section 2 presented the functional description of 10 inter-related components with their 90 operational control commands. The section totaled 160 pages.

Two weeks later this writer began training for a new career. He simply did not understand how to organize reference text.

Each component and its own operational control commands should have appeared in a separate section. This would have isolated the components for easy reference and allowed the reader to concentrate on one subject at a time.

Organizing Tutorial Text

Five principal rules can be applied to the organization of tutorial text.

1. *Introduce subjects in a logical sequence.* For example: Explain how data is stored before discussing how data is accessed.
2. *Centralize by topic.* For example: Decentralize related entities, such as programming statements, and describe them as they become appropriate to the operation under discussion.
3. *Arrange text in logical operational steps.* For example: Discuss special programming subjects, such as character conversion, as they become appropriate to the operation at hand.
4. *Avoid unnecessary detail.* For example: Limit discussions to the essentials and isolate information that is highly specialized.
5. *Avoid cross-references whenever possible.* For example: Arrange information so the reader can build on knowledge learned in previous sections and not have to flip back and forth through the manual.

A software design analyst once said:

Software technical writers are doing it all wrong! They are writing from the bottom up, starting with the smallest component and working up to the complete product. They should be writing from the top down, starting with the highest-level operations and working down to the smallest component. I will prove them wrong and write a tutorial the way I know one should be written.

Six months and 100 pages later, this analyst discovered his theory was wrong. The book had entered what is known as an endless loop in programming; it had no beginning and no end. He deposited his papers in the trash and went back to doing what he did best. He simply did not understand how to organize tutorial text.

Writing from the top down forces the reader to read the entire book in order to learn what the product is all about. Starting with the highest-level operations and working down to the smallest component expects the reader to grasp sophisticated concepts before learning the fundamentals. A successful tutorial begins at the beginning, explains the various components, and then teaches the reader how to use the product.

ORGANIZING THE TASK

Each computer company establishes its own standards for writing, editing, and production. It is important to observe these standards because they ensure consistency among the various product manuals.

In general:

- Every writing task requires a publications plan with scheduled completion dates for the writing, editing, review, and production phases.
- Every writing task requires a detailed outline.
- Every completed outline moves through at least one approval cycle.
- Every completed manual moves through at least two approval cycles.

Each computer company establishes completion dates for its software development. Almost without exception, the manuals must be ready to ship along with the software. Companies appear to operate in one of two ways.

Company A establishes a cutoff date for the program code, leaving writers with sufficient lead time to complete the manuals.

Company B establishes no cutoff date for the program code, leaving writers with insufficient lead time and always scrambling to make last-minute changes while the programmer codes and the printer waits.

If you work for Company A, your manual must be well organized from the very beginning because you are expected to produce the highest quality work at all times.

If you work for Company B, your manual must be well organized from the very beginning because you will run out of time and never have a chance to go back and restructure or rewrite.

3 / WRITING

A SOFTWARE

REFERENCE

MANUAL

A software reference manual is a complete description of a software product. This type of manual is required for almost every product developed within the computer industry. The reference manual is used constantly by the developing organization as well as its customers.

As new features are designed and incorporated into a product, the new features and their descriptions must be incorporated into the product reference manual. A well-organized and well-written manual can be easily maintained and updated; a poorly organized and poorly written manual is costly from the standpoint of time, resources, and customer satisfaction.

Designing and writing a software reference manual is a difficult task. But mechanics do exist. This chapter leads you through the logically ordered steps that help mechanize the design and preparation of a software reference manual.

KNOWING YOUR READERS

Before you start writing the manual, it is important to gain some insight into the audience. By asking yourself a few simple questions, you can analyze your readers and determine how you can satisfy their requirements.

Who Are the Readers?

You never know exactly who the readers are. They are not necessarily identifiable by the subject matter of the manual. For example:

> Will your reference manual describe a commercial programming language like COBOL? Your readers are probably application programmers.
>
> Will it describe a scientific programming language like FORTRAN? Your readers are probably scientific programmers.
>
> Will it describe an operating system? Your readers can be system programmers. They can also be application or scientific programmers looking for operating system interface information.

No matter what type of reference manual you are writing, you are always faced with this possibility:

> Your readers could be technicians or students trying to learn from your manual because it is the only documentation available to them.

How Knowledgeable Are the Readers?

You will never find the answer to this question. You have no way of knowing whether your readers are beginners or experts. They could have anywhere from 6 months to 30 years of professional experience. Programmers could be recent graduates, or they could be experts from other companies that have software entirely different from the software you are documenting.

Not knowing the readers' level of technical expertise complicates your task, and it is a reminder that you should never make assumptions.

> Never assume your readers are familiar with all of the terms. Even common terms like *record* and *file* can differ from one company to another.
>
> Never assume your readers are familiar with all of the software. The rules of a standard programming language, like COBOL, can differ from one type of hardware to another.

Never assume system programmers understand commercial applications, application programmers understand scientific programming, or scientific programmers understand commercial data processing.

Should any assumptions ever be made? *Yes.*

Always assume your readers are intelligent—intelligent enough to know when you are writing down to them.

How Will the Readers Use the Manual?

Now that you have a general idea of who your readers are and understand that they cannot be categorized as beginners or experts, it is important to think about how the readers will use the manual.

As its name implies, a reference manual is a manual that is used for reference. Readers are probably going to read out of context. This means that your manual must be organized so the material is easy to find. It does not matter who the readers are or how much they know or do not know; the value of your manual will depend on their being able to find what they are looking for and find it quickly.

FINDING THE INFORMATION FOR THE MANUAL

Finding the information for a software reference manual is almost as difficult as the writing itself. Information usually does exist. Unless you are a real veteran in the software technical writing field, you will never be asked to write a reference manual with only blank paper as a starting point.

You can gather information from four areas. We will discuss them in their order of importance.

Find the External Specifications

Unless the company opened its doors last month, external specifications written at the design level do exist. The specifications describe the product, its operation, and its use. They are written by a high-level analyst who is stating objectives so the staff can begin coding. These specifications have been known to reflect some or all of the following characteristics:

- They lack formal organization.
- They have errors of omission.
- They make assumptions.
- They are subject to change.

Specifications are meaningful to the analyst who wrote them, but they must be interpreted and organized so they are meaningful to you. Color-coding them by subject matter is a good way to start. If they have undefined terms, look them up and write down the definitions. If they reference components that are not familiar to you, find descriptions of these components in other manuals and record the page numbers; you will need to duplicate this type of information in your own manual. Anything that is not familiar to you might not be familiar to many of your readers.

The most important thing *not* to do is track down the author and start asking questions. Write down your questions.

Look for Informal Programming Notes

Now that you have a copy of the specifications, you can be sure programmers are working to develop product code. They will be operating at an amazing rate of speed. Remember, they also have deadlines to meet.

As long as programmers are coding, informal notes are laying around. Find out who these programmers are and ask for a copy of any notes they are maintaining. They will comply with your request because they are busy and do not want you hanging around.

These programming notes are critical. If they do not make sense to you now, they will later.

The most important thing *not* to do is return and start asking questions. Add these questions to your list.

Get the Program Listings

Program listings require notes. Companies cannot afford to have undocumented listings because new hires would spend too much time trying to interpret code. Get the listings. Maybe you will not understand them now, but you might later. Every bit of documentation counts!

The most important thing *not* to do is walk around with the listings and start asking questions. Add these questions to your list.

Ask Questions

Up to now asking questions has been discouraged. This is because questions have a way of answering themselves as you move through your sources of information.

By the time you reach this point, your list of questions will be organized and you can ask them all at one time. You will be surprised at how many questions you have crossed off your list.

A typical question is:

What default values are supplied by the system when parameters are omitted?

Programmers frequently are so intent on listing optional parameters that they forget to include default values.

In summary, ask questions only when you have all the available information and have gained some knowledge of your product.

GETTING ORGANIZED

The organization of a reference manual helps the readers to learn the product because the organization is, or at least should be, based on the organization of the product. Even though we know readers will read out of context, they should be able to open the manual to any section and pick up a thread of continuity.

You have all the information you need to get started on the outline. But where do you begin?

Begin with the Basic Concepts

Readers of your reference manual need the big picture and need it right away in Section 1. Every software product is made up of components that interact to form an operating unit. If any section can be considered totally mechanized, it is Section 1.

Section 1 would present the basic concepts in this general order:

1. an overview of the product
2. a brief description of each component that comprises the product
3. a description of the interaction of the components
4. an illustration of the interaction

Should Section 1 be written first or last? Many writers believe Section 1 should be written first because it gives them a better understanding of the product and helps them to write the other sections. Just as many writers believe Section 1 should be written last because only then can they have a complete understanding of the product.

You should do what is best for you.

Figure 3-1 shows a sample layout of a first section.

Look for Catalogs

Catalogs are series of logical groupings that can be found in any software product. By finding these catalogs, you have found the outline.

Are you writing a programming language reference manual? Here are some typical catalogs:

Attributes	Input/output processing
Coding conventions	Interface to other languages
Compilation	Language divisions
Data elements	Sample programs
Error messages	Statements
Functions	Subroutine calls

Are you writing an operating system reference manual? Here are some typical catalogs:

Control statements	Hardware configuration
Device handlers	Input operations
Disk organization	Instructions
Error messages	Interrupts

Libraries   Software configuration
Loading   Subroutines
Macros   System recovery
Output operations   Tape management
Program interface   Utility programs

SAMPLE SECTION 1

///
////////////////////////////////////// **Introductory material** /////////////////////////////////////
///

THE FIRST COMPONENT

///
///
///

Subheads would follow

THE NEXT COMPONENT

///
///
///

Subheads would follow

THE LAST COMPONENT

///
///
///

Subheads would follow

THE PROCESSING ENVIRONMENT

///
///
///

Illustration would follow

FIGURE 3-1 Sample Layout for Reference Manual Section 1

These logical groupings determine the organization and form the basic structure of the reference manual. Each grouping would break down into separate elements.

Figure 3-2 shows examples of catalog organization.

Organize Named Catalogs Alphabetically

A reference manual can be compared to an encyclopedia or a dictionary—it is strictly reference material. We can assume, then, that whenever possible the manual should reflect alphabetic order to make entries easy to locate. Catalogs that are named, such as programming statements, functions, instructions, and attributes, should be alphabetized.

Can you imagine what it would be like to use the dictionary if it were not in alphabetic order? Suppose dictionary words were grouped by logical categories such as verbs, adjectives, adverbs, and prepositions. Having a dictionary in logical order rather than alphabetic order would make the book difficult, if not impossible, to use. One would need a complete understanding of the language before being able to reference a single word. A logically organized dictionary would obviously defeat its very purpose.

Named catalogs appearing in logical order in a reference manual would present the same problem. If a manual described 100 named functions and documented the functions within their respective logical categories, each function would be theoretically buried. Readers could not locate a particular function without first knowing its category.

Acronyms present a special problem. Should you list the System Library function alphabetically by its name or by its acronym, SLY? These items can be listed by name with the acronym in parentheses, or listed by acronym. The important thing is to be consistent. If one function is listed by its acronym, all functions should be listed that way.

Names beginning with special characters, which are characters other than digits or letters, present another problem. Suppose you have two statements, one named END and another named %END. Although company standards vary, the END statement would usually be immediately followed by the %END statement. Names that consist entirely of special characters are usually positioned after alphabetic names and follow the order prescribed by your company.

Programming Language Reference Manual

SECTION 2. DATA ELEMENTS ◄——— A catalog concerning
the classification
Literal Constants   and description of
  Arithmetic Constant   all data elements
    Fixed Point Decimal Constant   used by the product
    Floating Point Decimal Constant
    Fixed Point Binary Constant
    Floating Point Binary Constant
  Character String Constant
Variables
  Computational Variable
    Arithmetic Variable
    String Variable
  Noncomputational Variable
    Entry Variable
    Label Variable
Aggregates
  Array
  Structure

Operating System Reference Manual

SECTION 3. LOADING PROCEDURES ◄——— A catalog concerning
the classification
Tape Loader   and description of
  Standard Tape Load   loading procedures
  Selective Tape Load
Disk Loader
  Standard Disk Load
  Selective Disk Load
Loading Input Commands
  Classification of Loading Input Commands
    ABORT Command
    ADD Command
    DELETE Command
    EDIT Command
    INITIALIZE Command
    LIST Command
    MERGE Command
    RESTART Command
    SORT Command
    WAIT Command
  Summary of Loading Input Commands

FIGURE 3-2 Sample Reference Manual Catalog Listings

When a logical order is also important, it can be shown along with the alphabetic order.

Suppose, for example, you have a section in your manual that deals with nine programming statements and it is important to let the readers know that three of them are control statements, three are input statements, and three are output statements. You could present them first in logical order, then discuss them in alphabetic order. Figure 3-3 illustrates this organization.

A paragraph head would introduce logical organization, and the text would reference a table similar to the following:

Table 3-1. Classification of Programming Statements

Category	Statement Name	Function
Control	Statement A	/////////
	Statement C	/////////
	Statement E	/////////
Input	Statement B	/////////
	Statement F	/////////
	Statement D	/////////
Output	Statement G	/////////
	Statement I	/////////
	Statement H	/////////

The next paragraph head would introduce the statements. Subsequent paragraph heads would introduce Statements A through I in alphabetic order.

FIGURE 3-3 Logical Organization

If your reviewers complain about the END statement being described before the START statement, remind them of the importance of alphabetic order. They will be the first to admit they go flipping through the section on statements looking for that *E* in *END statement* long before they methodically seek it out through the index.

INCLUDING RELATED INFORMATION

How many times have you mastered a programming language only to discover you could not run your program because the reference manual forgot to tell you how to get it past the operating system?

How many times have you worked with an operating system and discovered the reference manual forgot to describe the interface to the programming languages?

Did you end up going to another book to get this type of information? If a reader needs to use more than one book to gain an understanding of one product, something is wrong.

A product is usually influenced by various types of controls. Programming languages are controlled by the operating system. Operating systems are controlled by the hardware. A reference manual is obligated to tell the reader how to manage the equipment and operate successfully within this controlled environment.

If a reference manual included all related information, the book would be too heavy to carry. References to other manuals are obviously necessary. However, a good rule to remember is:

Always make the reference manual as self-contained as possible.

GENERATING EXAMPLES

Any reader will tell you a good example is worth three paragraphs. Every reference manual needs one or two complete sample executable programs. The examples should include the major features of the product; ideally, they would include all of the features. Readers frequently duplicate a sample program and execute it as a learning process. Running sample programs also provides a familiarity with the equipment.

But where do you get these examples? Designing and checking out good sample programs takes a lot of time, and you are working on a tight schedule. Besides, you are a writer and not necessarily an experienced programmer.

You will be doing yourself and your readers a big favor if you go to the experts for the examples. Programmers always have sample programs because they use them to check out their code. If their examples are dull statistical listings that neither you nor your readers would be interested in, try the quality assurance department. If you have no luck there, try the education department.

When all else fails, look around your own department. Good examples can always be found in your company's existing manuals. Take them—they are free. If you make some minor changes, they probably will never be recognized.

Programmers, by the way, are almost always willing to help a writer with a sample program. Why should you spend several days trying to debug a program that a programmer can correct in a few minutes?

When preparing examples, remember these four important rules:

1. Simple examples illustrate concepts; complex examples bury them.
2. Program output is important. If the program prints 17 pages of memory maps, it obviously is not necessary to include all of them. One or two partial pages, however, give the programmer some idea of what to expect during compilation or execution.
3. Program results are important. Sample programs should be realistic so computation results or printed reports can be included to show what actually happened.
4. Sample programs with errors are never going to execute. Run the program yourself to make sure it works. Always run it one last time from the final printed text to ensure against program code changes and typographical errors.

PREPARING THE OUTLINE

By now you have gathered all the necessary information, made valuable contacts, and have enough material to develop a complete outline for your reference manual.

Let us assume you have been assigned the task of writing a reference manual for a new programming language. The specifications have provided descriptions of the following:

- three modules that comprise the product (source program, operation control process, and object file)
- syntax and explanations of eight statements:

   two statements that delimit the program (BEGIN and END)

   one statement that defines a table of constant values (TABLE)

   four statements that perform arithmetic operations (ADD, SUBTRACT, MULTIPLY, and DIVIDE)

   one statement that performs condition testing (IF)
- coding requirements
- suggestions for efficient programming

Figure 3-4 is a sample outline for this type of product.

Once you have generated the outline, you have completed the most important part of your writing assignment.

The beginning of this chapter emphasized the importance of organization to the reference manual. A novel is read, a newspaper is scanned, a dissertation is studied, but a reference manual is used.

Ask yourself these final questions about the outline:

1. Does it begin with the big picture?
2. Is every topic included?
3. Does every topic have a principal home?
4. Are topics organized so the reader will not have to switch back and forth between sections?
5. Is the information broken down into logical units so the next writer will be able to add update material?

If you can answer yes to each of these questions, the outline will probably be approved. You are ready to begin writing.

SECTION 1. INTRODUCTION TO OURLANGUAGE

OURLANGUAGE Components
   Source Program   ⎫
   Operation Control Process   ⎬ The three modules
   Object File   ⎭
OURLANGUAGE Processing ⟶ Module interaction

SECTION 2. LANGUAGE COMPONENTS

Data Reference   ⎫
   Data Class
   Data Name
Constants
   Numeric Constants
   Character Constants   ⎬ Information derived from
   Figurative Constants   various parts of the
Relational Operators   specification
Tables
   Table Structure
   Subscripting
Punctuation   ⎭

SECTION 3. OURLANGUAGE STATEMENTS

Statement Classification   ⎫
   Program Delimiters
   Table Declaration   ⎬ Functional descriptions
   Arithmetic Operations   of the eight statements
   Condition Testing   ⎭
Statement Descriptions   ⎫
   ADD Statement
   BEGIN Statement
   DIVIDE Statement
   END Statement   ⎬ Alphabetized descriptions
   IF Statement   of the eight statements
   MULTIPLY Statement
   SUBTRACT Statement
   TABLE Statement   ⎭   ⟶

FIGURE 3-4 Sample Reference Manual Outline

SECTION 4. PROGRAM PREPARATION

OURLANGUAGE Coding
   Comment Lines
   Continuation Lines   } Specific breakdown for
   Blank Lines   easy reference
Program Structure

SECTION 5. PROGRAMMING EFFICIENCY

Conserving Storage
Maintaining Mode Consistency   } Specific breakdown
Organizing Table Entries   for emphasis

SECTION 6. COMPILATION AND EXECUTION

Program Compilation
   DEBUG Parameter   } Alphabetized breakdown
   LIST Parameter   for index and contents
   SUPPRESS Parameter   reference
Program Execution
Program Output

SECTION 7. SAMPLE PROGRAMS ⟶ Programs would include
                                        table subscripting, an
                                        arithmetic operation,
                                        and condition testing

FIGURE 3-4 (cont.)

PREPARING THE TEXT

Software technical writers, just like other technical writers, are expected to have language skills. Being able to write—and to write well—is the basic part of this discipline. The highly specialized part involves selecting the right words and producing organized text from specifications.

Selecting the Right Words

Ordinary words that once seemed to be the same can carry different connotations when applied to software. *Use* and *usage* are not the same, nor are *transmit* and *send.* Simple words like *move, procedure, perform, function, signal,* and *item* can mean many things to many software products.

The word *perform* has a very special meaning in the COBOL language. You would be taking an unnecessary risk to say COBOL performs a variety of functions. The generic term *perform* could be confused with the PER-FORM verb in the COBOL language.

The word *function* has a very special meaning in the PL/I language. You would not want to say PL/I performs a variety of functions. The generic term *functions* could be confused with the specialized builtin functions that are an integral part of the PL/I language.

The word *section* has a special meaning in many languages. If you told the reader to write a section of code to handle some particular operation for one of these languages, it would not be clear whether the word *section* was being used as a generic or a technical term.

When selecting a word, make sure it does not conflict with a term that is unique to the software.

Producing Organized Text from Specifications

The most difficult part of software technical writing is being able to read a specification and to immediately establish a writing approach. After you have read 10 or 15 specifications and produced successful reference manuals from them, the approach becomes somewhat automatic. When you are reading the first specification and producing the first reference manual, the approach is not all that easy to find.

Figure 3-5 illustrates writing reference text from a specification. The illustration is divided into four parts:

Part 1 is a small portion of an oversimplified specification that describes four statements of a hypothetical compiler.

Part 2 is a sample outline for the text.

Part 3 is a list of obvious questions that would need to be asked.

Part 4 is a sample write-up in reference manual format.

The write-up is a suggested approach. A good exercise would be to read part 1, use the outline in part 2, make up answers to part 3, and then do your own write-up. Be sure to introduce and define terms and components before referencing them, and arrange the text so information can be easily located.

A WORD ABOUT SCHEDULES

Schedules for software reference manuals are usually prepared entirely by the writer—entirely, that is, except for something called the release date. The release date is determined by some higher authority and represents the date the software is being shipped along with your printed manual.

You can schedule all the time you need for your reference manual as long as it is printed and sitting on the shelf by the release date. If you believe your manual should have a one-year writing schedule and the release date is 6 months down the road, you will be scheduling the writing time for around 4½ months. This will leave sufficient time for production, printing, and distribution.

Software reference manual writers generally fall into one of two categories:

Category 1 The optimist functions in a totally relaxed environment during the first half of the schedule, fraternizing with co-workers and convinced the release date will slip. During the last half of the schedule, this writer discovers that the release date has not changed. Panic sets in, and the reference manual is written at the speed of light, ending up with little or no quality.

Category 2 The realist panics during the first half of the schedule, convinced that the release date will not change and might even be pushed forward. During the last half of the schedule, this writer finds time to incorporate quality.

If you are a category 1 writer, try to move up to category 2. If you are a category 2 writer, stay there. Software technical writing is a pressurized business, and panic should be planned for the beginning—never the end—of the schedule and its notorious release date.

Part 1. A Sample Specification

Statements

The ARRANGE compiler has two declarative statements (BEGIN and END) and two imperative statements (MOVE and DISPLAY). The statements are used in display modules. BEGIN and END act as delimiters, MOVE arranges text, and DISPLAY displays the data on the terminal.

Syntax

BEGIN must be the first statement in the module. The BEGIN statement parameter must match the END statement module-number.

        BEGIN <module-number>

        <module-number> = 1-37

END should be the last statement and must match the BEGIN parameter. If the statement is omitted, the compiler supplies it and issues a warning.

        END <module-number>

        <module-number> = 1-37

MOVE takes data from memory and places it in proper positions in a buffer for display. The first character of a <data-item> is positioned for display in COLUMN <number>.

        MOVE <data-item> TO COLUMN <number>

        <data-item> = name of item defined in the Declarations area

        <number>   = 1-73

DISPLAY displays the item. The statement must follow at least one MOVE. Only one DISPLAY statement is allowed in a module.

        DISPLAY

Example

        BEGIN 3
        MOVE EMP-NO TO COLUMN 10
        MOVE DEPT TO COLUMN 4C
        DISPLAY
        END 3

                                                        ⟶

FIGURE 3-5 Writing Reference Manual Text from a Sample Specification

Part 2. A Sample Outline

ARRANGE STATEMENTS

    BEGIN Statement
    DISPLAY Statement
    END Statement
    MOVE Statement
    Sample Display Module

Part 3. Questions to Be Asked

What is the maximum number of MOVE statements that can be issued between the delimiters?

Can module numbers be duplicated?

What happens if column numbers are duplicated or overlapped?

For multiple MOVE statements, do column numbers have to be specified in ascending numeric order?

What warning message is issued when the END statement is omitted?

Where does data-item come from?

Part 4. A Sample Reference Manual Write-up from the Specification

ARRANGE STATEMENTS

ARRANGE statements are used to build program modules that display data on a terminal. A statement consists of the reserved words of the ARRANGE language in combination with programmer-supplied elements.

ARRANGE statements are divided into two functional categories:

- declarative— statements that supply the compiler with information essential to the compilation

- imperative — statements that specify unconditional actions to be performed at execute time.

An ARRANGE module has two declarative statements; both are required:

    BEGIN

    END
                                                         ⟶

FIGURE 3-5 (cont.)

An ARRANGE module has two imperative statements; both are required:

MOVE

DISPLAY

Each of these statements has a prescribed position in relation to each other.

• A BEGIN statement is the first statement in the module.

• One or more MOVE statements follow the BEGIN statement.

• One DISPLAY statement follows the last MOVE statement.

• An END statement is the last statement in the module.

For example:

```
BEGIN . . .
MOVE . . .
MOVE . . .
   .
   .
DISPLAY
END . . .
```

BEGIN Statement

The BEGIN statement is the module entry point. BEGIN statement syntax is:

BEGIN module-number

where

module-number

is an integer from 1 through 37. Module numbers cannot be duplicated within a program. Each program is limited to 37 modules.

Module-number must match the *module-number* specified on the associated END statement.

The BEGIN statement must be the first statement in the module and must have an END statement with a matching module number.

DISPLAY Statement

The DISPLAY statement takes the data that has been positioned in the buffer by one or more MOVE statements and displays that data on one line of the terminal screen. DISPLAY statement syntax is:

DISPLAY $\longrightarrow$

FIGURE 3-5 (cont.)

GOSHEN COLLEGE LIBRARY
GOSHEN, INDIANA

The statement consists of the single word DISPLAY.

The DISPLAY statement must immediately follow the last MOVE statement. You can include only one DISPLAY statement in a module.

END Statement

The END statement terminates the module. END statement syntax is:

> END module-number

>> where

>>> module-number

>>>> is an integer from 1 through 37. *Module-number* must match the *module-number* specified on the associated BEGIN statement.

The END statement must be the last statement in the module. If you omit this statement, the compiler supplies the statement and issues the warning message W-END STATEMENT MISSING.

MOVE Statement

The MOVE statement takes an item of data from memory and positions it in a buffer for display by the DISPLAY statement. MOVE statement syntax is:

> MOVE data-item TO COLUMN number

>> where

>>> data-item

>>>> is the name of the invoice item that has been entered by the terminal operator. The data item must be an item that you have defined in the Declarations area of the program.

>>> number

>>>> is an integer from 1 through 73. The number represents the column number where the first character of *data-item* is to be positioned.

Each MOVE statement establishes column positioning for one data item. The length of the data item determines exactly how many column positions the data item occupies. If you move a 10-character data item to column 20, for example, the first character of the data item will appear in column 20 and the last character will appear in column 29.

You can include any number of MOVE statements in a single module provided characters do not extend beyond column 73. You cannot, for example, move

———>

FIGURE 3-5 (cont.)

a 5-character data item to column 70 or a 30-character data item to column 50.

If you have multiple MOVE statements in a module, you must not overlap column positions. If the first MOVE statement moves a 10-character data item to column 20, a second MOVE statement cannot move a data item to column 27; the data items will overlap and produce an E-OVERLAP error message.

Multiple MOVE statements need not be coded so that column numbers appear in ascending numeric order. The first MOVE statement can move a data item to column 70, and the second MOVE statement can move a data item to column 1.

Spacing is an important consideration. Calculate the amount of space needed between displayed items. If the first MOVE statement moves a 10-character data item to column 20 and the second MOVE statement moves a data item to column 30, the two items will be adjacent with no intervening space.

Sample Display Module

The following sample module positions three data items called ID, DEPART-MENT, and LOCATION. ID has 4 characters, DEPARTMENT has 10 characters, and LOCATION has 3 characters.

```
BEGIN 14
MOVE ID TO COLUMN 5
MOVE DEPARTMENT TO COLUMN 11
MOVE LOCATION TO COLUMN 23
DISPLAY
END 14
```

If ID = 1234, DEPARTMENT = ACCOUNTING, and LOCATION = 498, output from this program would appear as:

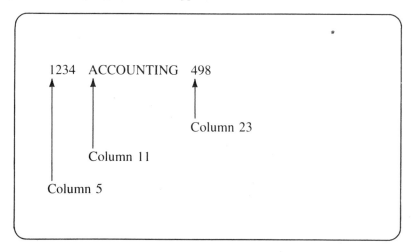

FIGURE 3-5 (cont.)

4 / WRITING

A SOFTWARE

USER MANUAL

A software user manual is tutorial. This type of manual is not a comprehensive description of a software product; it is usually a supplement to existing documentation.

A user manual serves three important functions:

- It provides practical information when formal classroom instruction is not available.
- It helps the inexperienced to get started quickly.
- It helps the experienced to become productive quickly.

Designing and writing a software user manual is a task that is generally reserved for the more experienced writer. The task invites creativity, assumes a working knowledge of the product, and demands objectivity. But mechanics do exist. This chapter leads you through the logically ordered steps that help mechanize the writing of a software user manual.

KNOWING YOUR READERS

Before you start writing the user manual, it is important to gain some insight into the audience. By asking yourself a few simple questions, you can analyze your readers and determine how you can satisfy their requirements.

Who Are the Readers?

You know exactly who the readers are. The readers are automatically identified when the need for the user manual is recognized by your organization.

Perhaps your organization has developed an extremely complicated programming language and discovers customer programming staff members are having trouble getting started. Local and site analysts are constantly responding to customer telephone calls for help.

Perhaps your organization has developed a sophisticated data base management system and discovers customer design analysts need specialized information that does not appear in the various reference manuals.

When the need for a user manual arises and you get the assignment, you know exactly who your readers are.

How Knowledgeable Are the Readers?

You know the answer to this question, too. With rare exceptions, tutorial text is directed toward one level of expertise.

If you are writing for experienced analysts and programmers, you would not define familiar terms unless the terms were unique to the product or the operating environment; your readers do not have time to read what they already know. If you are writing for less experienced analysts and programmers, you would go out of your way to define all terms.

When writing a user manual, you make many assumptions. Remember to state these assumptions in the preface so readers will know exactly where they stand.

How Will the Readers Use the Manual?

Now that you know exactly who your readers are and understand that they fit into a particular category, it is important to think about how the readers will use the manual.

Initially readers are going to read in context, beginning on page 1 and continuing through to the end. They will be operating in a *learn-as-you-go* mode. This means that your manual must be organized so the material reflects continuity and a definite hierarchy in its presentation. The value of your manual will depend on how quickly the readers are able to grasp the basic ideas and build up to the most sophisticated concepts.

FINDING THE INFORMATION FOR THE MANUAL

Finding information for a software user manual is not too difficult, but finding the right kind of information depends a great deal on your own personal knowledge of the product. If you are not familiar with the product, it is important for you to learn it quickly and use it as you proceed through the writing phase.

You can gather information from three areas. We will discuss them in their order of importance.

Use the Software Reference Manual

We have determined that a user manual is written when the need arises. This implies that some form of reference material already exists.

> If a reference manual does exist, all information is available, waiting to be reorganized and presented in tutorial format.

> If a reference manual does not exist, someone is probably in the process of writing it and will make the material available to you in stages.

The most important thing to do is ask questions about anything that is not entirely clear to you. If you start writing a user manual with misconceptions, you will carry them throughout the book and end up doing extensive rewrites.

Talk to Customer Support Analysts

Software technical writers are not always fortunate enough to be able to talk to customers. For that reason, it is important to talk to individuals who do. These are the customer support analysts who handle customer problems and understand their needs.

Spend as much time as possible with these analysts. Make definite appointments with them, ask their opinions, consider their ideas, and ask them to read your manual section by section. Their input is invaluable.

Talk to Programmers

By the time you start writing a user manual, programmers who worked on the product are busy working on other projects. You need to talk to them, so try not to let them get away. Quality assurance programmers who tested the product before its release are very important contacts; find them while the product is fresh in their minds. Teachers in the education department are also excellent contacts because they usually have course material they are willing to share; if you produce a good user manual, they can spend less time teaching the basics and more time teaching the extremely complex concepts.

Again, make definite appointments with these individuals, ask their opinions, and consider their ideas. They probably will not be receptive to reading your manual section by section, but it never hurts to ask.

GETTING ORGANIZED

The organization of a user manual teaches the reader how to use the product. Readers are going to start out reading from beginning to end, so continuity is the key to success.

You have established all the contacts you need to get started on the outline. But where do you begin?

Begin with the Basic Concepts

Readers of a user manual are no different from the readers of a reference manual. They, too, need the big picture and need it right away in Section 1. Hopefully, the existing or evolving reference manual is a good one because it will make your task easier.

Everything that appeared in Section 1 of the reference manual can appear in Section 1 of your user manual, with two important changes.

1. *Remove extraneous detail.* Tell readers only what they need to know to get started.
2. *Include product philosophy.* Tell readers why the product was developed, what it can do for them, and, if appropriate, how the product compares to similar products they might be using.

Figure 4-1 shows a sample layout of a first section.

Look for Features

Features are the individual capabilities of the product. By finding the features, you have found the outline.

Are you writing a programming language user manual? Here are some typical features:

Describing files	Writing subroutines
Creating files	Compressing files
Modifying files	Creating a data base
Linking files	Establishing checkpoints

Are you writing an operating system user manual? Here are some typical features:

Analyzing system activity	Loading the initialize program
Monitoring interrupts	Recovering the data base
Cataloging passwords	Defining log operations
Using debugging tools	Assigning devices

These features determine the organization and form the basic structure of the user manual. Each feature would break down into separate elements.

The features of a user manual correspond to the catalogs of a reference manual. Although they differ slightly from each other, they are used for similar purposes. Catalogs establish the basic organization of a reference manual; features establish the basic organization of a user manual.

Figure 4-2 shows examples of feature organization.

SAMPLE SECTION 1

///
// Introductory material //
///

THE HARDWARE ENVIRONMENT

///
///
///

Subheads would follow

THE SOFTWARE ENVIRONMENT

///
///
///

Subheads would follow

THE PROCESSING ENVIRONMENT

///
///
///

Illustration would follow

THE OPERATING ENVIRONMENT

///
///
///

Subheads would follow

FIGURE 4-1 Sample Layout for User Manual Section 1

Organize Logically

Unlike a reference manual, a user manual is not organized alphabetically. People do not learn in alphabetic order; they learn in
logically ordered steps, beginning with the basics and building

up to the most complex procedures. If you are writing a programming language user manual, for example, you would describe the various programming statements in logical order.

Programming Language User Manual

SECTION 2. DESIGNING THE DATA BASE ◄——— A feature dealing
                                          exclusively with
Defining Data Base Structure   data base design
  File Organizations
    Sequential Files
    Relative Files
    Indexed Files
  Record Formats
    Format A
    Format W
    Format D
Establishing Security
  Assigning Passwords
  Modifying Passwords
  Deleting Passwords
Incorporating Validity Checks

Operating System User Manual

SECTION 3. LOADING PROCEDURES ◄——— A feature dealing
                                     exclusively with
Understanding the Equipment   loading procedures
Writing the Tape Object Loader
  A Standard Tape Load
  A Selective Tape Load
    Setting Program IDs
    Reading Driver Code
Writing the Disk Object Loader
  A Standard Disk Load
  A Selective Disk Load
Using Control Records
  Altering Switch Settings
  Setting Table Pointers
  Accessing the Control Directory

FIGURE 4-2 Sample User Manual Feature Listings

Even though the *E* in *END statement* is near the beginning of the alphabet, you would not discuss the statement until after you had discussed the START statement.

Each section of the manual is based on an understanding of the preceding section. For example:

- If you are writing a programming language user manual, you would discuss file organization before telling the programmer how to build alternate key files.
- If you are writing an operating system user manual, you would discuss disk organization before telling the analyst how to best utilize disk storage.

INCLUDING RELATED INFORMATION

A user manual should be completely self-contained. It is important to indicate where more detailed information can be located, but the reader should never have to put the manual down and go looking for other documents. Scattered references to other books defeat the very purpose of a user manual. For example:

- If you are writing a programming language user manual, include necessary operating system information.
- If you are writing an operating system user manual, include necessary hardware information.

GENERATING EXAMPLES

Examples represent the most important aspect of a user manual. Entering and executing examples while reading the manual are comparable to on-the-job training. Partial examples can be interspersed with the text, but a complete executable program should be shown at the end of each feature being discussed.

Where do you get the examples? You should generate them yourself, with any necessary guidance from your contacts. If you create your own examples, you will be sure to make mistakes, and this gives you an opportunity to point out the pitfalls your readers will encounter.

When preparing examples, remember these four important rules:

1. Use examples that are meaningful and not too complex. In some cases it is necessary to give the readers information out of order about the topic at hand to allow them to use material at the beginning. A typical example is FORTRAN, where the complicated FORMAT statement is too difficult to include early but too basic to be avoided. Supply this type of information so that readers can copy it for use until you reach a more suitable place for the discussion.

2. Include appropriate input and output so that readers can see what is happening.

3. Include any operating requirements.

   If you are writing a programming language user manual, be sure to include any necessary operating system commands that are needed for successful execution.

   If you are writing an operating system user manual, be sure to include any hardware considerations that affect the processing environment.

4. Make sure the programs are accurate and will execute successfully.

The various techniques that can be used for preparing user manual examples include color, contrasting type font, and shading. Figure 4-3 gives an example of the shading technique. Information to be entered by the reader is shaded to contrast with system responses that are not.

PREPARING THE OUTLINE

Unlike writing a reference manual, gathering information is not the most important part of your writing assignment. Before you even begin an outline for a user manual, you should be using the product. You are not describing now—you are teaching.

While you are using the product, it is a good idea to try things you know are not only wrong but even ridiculous. If, for example, the reference manual mildly cautions the programmer against performing a certain function during some phase

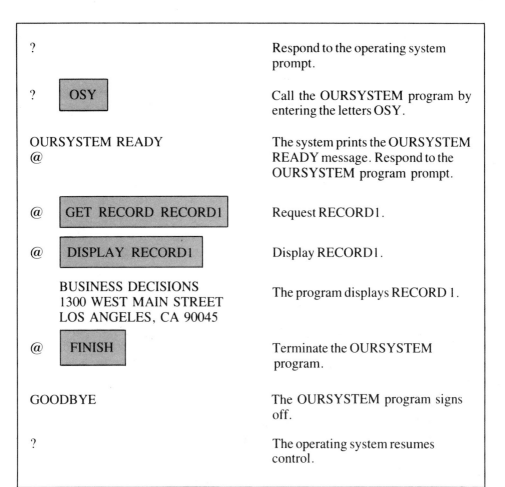

?		Respond to the operating system prompt.
?	OSY	Call the OURSYSTEM program by entering the letters OSY.
OURSYSTEM READY @		The system prints the OURSYSTEM READY message. Respond to the OURSYSTEM program prompt.
@	GET RECORD RECORD1	Request RECORD1.
@	DISPLAY RECORD1	Display RECORD1.
	BUSINESS DECISIONS 1300 WEST MAIN STREET LOS ANGELES, CA 90045	The program displays RECORD 1.
@	FINISH	Terminate the OURSYSTEM program.
GOODBYE		The OURSYSTEM program signs off.
?		The operating system resumes control.

FIGURE 4-3 Shading Technique

of the operation, try it—even if you bring down the entire system.

Let us assume you have been assigned the task of writing a user manual for the programming language that was outlined in Figure 3-4 of Chapter 3. Figure 4-4 gives a sample outline for the same product.

Ask yourself these final questions about the outline:

1. Does it begin with the big picture?

2. Are the major features included?

3. Are the features presented in an order that ranges from basic to complex?

If you can answer yes to each of these questions, the outline will probably be approved. You are ready to begin writing.
Software user manual writers are notorious for uncovering
program bugs. These are the writers who are playing the role of
customer, doing the expected and the unexpected, and finding

SECTION 1.   INTRODUCTION TO OURLANGUAGE

OURLANGUAGE Components
   Designing the Source Program
   Interfacing the Operation Control
     Process   } The three modules
   Storing the Object File
OURLANGUAGE Processing

SECTION 2.   PROGRAM STRUCTURE

Program Organization
Language Elements
   Establishing Data Class   Setting up the program
   Declaring Program Constants   structure, which will
Coding Conventions   } be used as an ongoing
   Source Program Entries   example and be continued
   Continuation Lines   throughout the manual
   Comment Lines
   Blank Lines

SECTION 3.   ARITHMETIC OPERATIONS

Arithmetic Expressions
   Arithmetic Operators
   Simple Arithmetic Expressions
   Complex Arithmetic Expressions
   Evaluating Expressions
Arithmetic Statements   } Illustrating the use of
   Addition of Items   all arithmetic statements
   Subtraction of Items
   Multiplication of Items
   Division of Items
Sample Arithmetic Programs   ⟶

FIGURE 4-4 Sample User Manual Outline

SECTION 4. CONDITION OPERATIONS

Condition Expressions
   Relation Testing
      Comparing Numeric and
         Character Data
      Comparing Numeric Data Items
         Items with Equal Lengths
         Items with Unequal Lengths
   Class Testing
Sample Condition Programs

} Illustrating the use of the condition IF statement

SECTION 5. TABLE HANDLING

Defining Tables
Storing Table Elements
Searching Tables
   Using Subscripts
   Setting Value Ranges
Sample Table Handling Programs

} Illustrating the use and manipulation of tables

SECTION 6. COMPILATION AND EXECUTION

Compiling the Source Program
   LIST Parameter
   DEBUG Parameter
   SUPPRESS Parameter
Compilation Output Listings
Executing the Source Program
Sample Input File Structures

} Compiling and executing a program that now includes all features

FIGURE 4-4 (cont.)

out how the software really performs when it is at the mercy of both the expert and the novice.

PREPARING THE TEXT

Before you can begin to write a software user manual, you are faced with two prerequisites: learning the product and understanding how the reader is going to use the product.

If your assignment was to write a user manual on how to drive a car, you would not want to begin the actual writing until you had driven a car yourself. You could manage the outline because you would be including such topics as starting the car, operating the gear shift, and so forth. But you still need to drive the car.

If your reader was going to use your manual for driving a car in the Indianapolis 500, you could probably still manage the outline; but you are faced with an entirely different situation.

Using the product several weeks before generating any text is always a good idea. If you cannot learn how to use the product by reading the existing reference material, you can be sure the customers are in trouble. Turn to the customer support analysts for help.

Figure 3-5 in Chapter 3 presented a sample specification and included a write-up that would be appropriate for a reference manual. A good exercise would be to change that write-up into one that would be appropriate for a user manual. Be sure to introduce subjects in a logical sequence and arrange the text so that it teaches the reader how to use the product.

Figure 4-5 is an example of one way to do this.

SCHEDULES ARE ALWAYS REQUIRED

Some organizations do not require software user manuals to be shipped along with the software. If you happen to work for one of those organizations, the user manual, unlike the reference manual, will not have to be sitting on the shelf by the release date for that software.

This only *sounds* like encouraging news.

Software user manuals are expected to be written within a reasonable period of time. Once you have prepared the schedule and it has been approved, you are tied to your own personal release date.

So you face one of two possible situations:

You must meet a schedule that is tied to a software release date. Your organization and its customers are depending on it.

You must meet a schedule that is tied to your own personal release date. Your next raise is depending on it.

This write-up was generated from the sample
specification shown in Figure 3-5 of Chapter 3.

WRITING MODULES FOR DISPLAYING DATA

After you have defined all of the data items in the Declarations area of the
program, you can code modules to have data displayed on the terminal. Each
module displays data on one line of the terminal screen.

Display modules consist of four ARRANGE statements that appear in the following order:

BEGIN   —   establishes the module entry point.

MOVE   —   positions data for terminal display.

DISPLAY —   displays the data.

END   —   terminates the module.

Delimiting the Modules

Begin each module with a BEGIN statement and supply a module number. The
module number must be an integer from 1 through 37 and must be unique
within all program modules.

BEGIN module-number

For example:

BEGIN 1
.
.
.
.
.

End each module with an END statement and duplicate the module number
you assigned to the associated BEGIN statement.

END module-number

                     ⟶

FIGURE 4-5 Writing User Manual Text from a Sample Specification

For example:

BEGIN 1

.
.
.

END 1

If you omit the END statement, the compiler supplies one and issues a warning message W-END STATEMENT MISSING. For documentation purposes, it is good programming practice to always include an END statement.

Positioning the Data for Display

Follow each BEGIN statement with one or more MOVE statements. These statements take named items of data from memory and position them in a buffer for subsequent display on a terminal screen.

MOVE data-item TO COLUMN number

Supply the name of a data item that you have defined in the Declarations area of the program. Also supply a column number from 1 through 73; this number is the column number where the first character of the data item is to be positioned.

For example:

BEGIN 1

MOVE EMPLOYEE-ID TO COLUMN 1 ← The first character of
                                EMPLOYEE-ID is positioned
.   for display in column 1.
.
.   If EMPLOYEE-ID is 4
                                characters long, the item
END 1   is positioned for display
                                in columns 1 through 4.

⟶

FIGURE 4-5 (cont.)

You can have multiple MOVE statements provided the characters do not extend beyond column 73. For example:

BEGIN 1

MOVE EMPLOYEE-ID TO COLUMN 1

MOVE EMPLOYEE-NAME TO COLUMN 36

MOVE DEPARTMENT TO COLUMN 60 ◄— DEPARTMENT must not
.   exceed 14 characters
.   because it would then
.   extend beyond column 73.

END 1

Avoid Column Overlap

If your MOVE statements cause two characters to occupy the same column position, the compiler issues an E-OVERLAP error message. If data-item EMPLOYEE-ID in the following example is a 4-character field, overlap occurs:

MOVE EMPLOYEE-ID TO COLUMN 1 ◄— Extends through column 4

MOVE EMPLOYEE-NAME TO COLUMN 4 ◄— Overlaps column 4

Allow for Spacing Between Data Items

If your MOVE statements do not allow for spacing between data items, values will be adjacent when displayed on the terminal screen. The following statements will provide no spacing between the 4-character field EMPLOYEE-ID and EMPLOYEE-NAME:

MOVE EMPLOYEE-ID TO COLUMN 1 ◄— Extends through column 4

MOVE EMPLOYEE-NAME TO COLUMN 5 ◄— Begins in column 5

—►

FIGURE 4-5 (cont.)

Displaying the Data

Include a DISPLAY statement after the last MOVE statement. The DISPLAY statement causes the positioned data items to be displayed on the terminal screen. The statement consists of the single word

DISPLAY

You can include only one DISPLAY statement in a module. For example:

```
BEGIN 1
MOVE EMPLOYEE-ID TO COLUMN 1
MOVE EMPLOYEE-NAME TO COLUMN 36
MOVE DEPARTMENT TO COLUMN 60
DISPLAY
END 1
```

Sample Display Modules

The following example is an ARRANGE module for displaying two fields:

```
BEGIN 2
MOVE DEPARTMENT TO COLUMN 4
MOVE LOCATION TO COLUMN 16
DISPLAY
END 2
```

where

DEPARTMENT is a 10-character field and LOCATION is a 2-character field.

The two fields would be displayed on one line of the terminal screen.

FIGURE 4-5 (cont.)

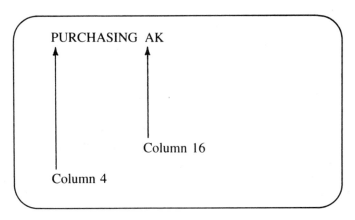

The following example is an ARRANGE module for displaying three fields:

```
BEGIN 3
MOVE DEPARTMENT TO COLUMN 10
MOVE DEPT-CODE TO COLUMN 2
MOVE LOCATION TO COLUMN 22
DISPLAY
END 3
```

where

DEPARTMENT is a 10-character field, DEPT-CODE is a 3-character field, and LOCATION is a 2-character field.

The three fields would be displayed on one line of the terminal screen.

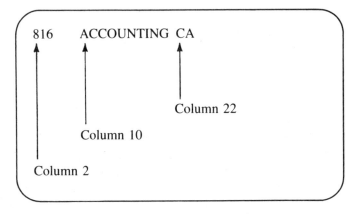

FIGURE 4-5 (cont.)

5/STRUCTURING

TECHNIQUES

What is structure?

The dictionary defines structure as something arranged in a definite pattern of organization. We already know how important organization is to software manuals. The underlying structure of the text itself is just as important.

This chapter discusses techniques that help to structure your software manuals for usability.

ESTABLISHING STRUCTURED PARAGRAPH AND SECTION HEADS

Paragraph and section heads are titles that precede and identify subsequent blocks of text. These heads clearly define the organizational breakdown of the manual.

The positioning and content of heads can affect the structure of a software manual. The next two heads in this chapter introduce the techniques for establishing paragraph and section heads.

Balancing paragraph heads is nothing more than accurately dividing information into topics. If you think back to grade school, you will remember how you used to make outlines. They went something like this:

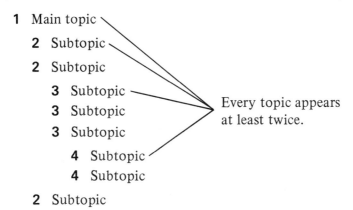

1 Main topic

  2 Subtopic

  2 Subtopic

    3 Subtopic

    3 Subtopic   Every topic appears at least twice.

    3 Subtopic

      4 Subtopic

      4 Subtopic

  2 Subtopic

1 Main topic

These simple little outlines still apply, but how many times have you seen an unbalanced paragraph head in a software manual? Figure 5-1 is a typical example.

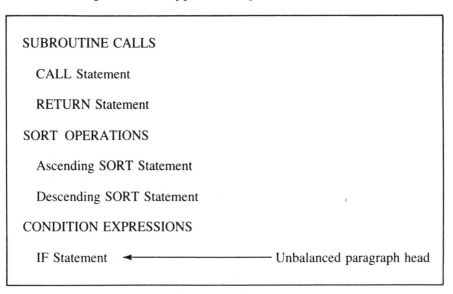

SUBROUTINE CALLS

  CALL Statement

  RETURN Statement

SORT OPERATIONS

  Ascending SORT Statement

  Descending SORT Statement

CONDITION EXPRESSIONS

  IF Statement ◄————————— Unbalanced paragraph head

FIGURE 5-1 An Unbalanced Paragraph Head

This sample outline is saying the topic *Subroutine calls* is divided into two parts, the topic *Sort operations* is divided into two parts, and the topic *Condition expressions* is divided into one part. Logically, nothing can be divided into one part.

The sample outline with its unbalanced paragraph head reflects clear organization and complete information, but it does not reflect good structure.

The outline with the unbalanced paragraph head can be easily repaired. Figure 5-2 offers two ways to correct it.

Example 1

SUBROUTINE CALLS

  CALL Statement

  RETURN Statement

SORT OPERATIONS

  Ascending SORT Statement

  Descending SORT Statement

CONDITION EXPRESSIONS

Example 2

SUBROUTINE CALLS (CALL, RETURN)

  CALL Statement

  RETURN Statement

SORT OPERATIONS (SORT)

  Ascending SORT Statement

  Descending SORT Statement

CONDITION EXPRESSIONS (IF)

FIGURE 5-2 Balanced Paragraph Heads

Looking at example 1, many writers will argue that it is more important for the IF statement to appear than to have balanced paragraph heads. They will also be concerned because the IF statement will not appear in the table of contents. Example 2 is one way out of this situation.

Avoiding Empty Heads

A section head immediately followed by a paragraph head with no intervening text is an empty section head.

A paragraph head immediately followed by another paragraph head with no intervening text is an empty paragraph head.

Figure 5-3 shows a page of text with an empty section and paragraph head.

The empty section head is announcing the beginning of a completely new section about which the writer has nothing of interest to tell the readers.

The empty paragraph head indicates that the writer wanted to divide the two types of sort operations into two separate paragraph heads (ascending sort and descending sort) and collect them under the single paragraph head *Sort operations (SORT)*. But notice that the paragraph head *Sort operations (SORT)* introduces nothing but empty space.

If section and paragraph heads are important enough to appear, they are important enough to carry introductory text. This introductory text serves two purposes:

1. It summarizes the subsequent information for the reader.
2. It provides an area for highlighting update information.

Figure 5-4 shows the same page without the empty heads.

WRITING IN PARALLEL

Writing in parallel is writing in a consistent style. Consistency includes the following:

- using the same voice, either all active or all passive
- using the same construction, either all complete sentences or all sentence fragments.

SECTION 5

OURSYSTEM STATEMENTS

◄──────────Empty section head

SUBROUTINE CALLS

Subroutine calls transfer control to a subroutine and effect a return to the main logic path of the XYZ program . . . .

CALL Statement

The CALL statement unconditionally transfers control to the subroutine. The statement consists of the CALL . . . .

RETURN Statement

The RETURN statement provides the linkage back to the main path of the XYZ program. The statement consists . . . .

SORT OPERATIONS (SORT)

◄──────────Empty paragraph head

Ascending SORT Statement

The ascending SORT statement arranges information in ascending order according to the internal code of the . . . .

Descending SORT Statement

The descending SORT statement arranges information in descending order according to the internal code of the . . . .

FIGURE 5-3 An Empty Section and Paragraph Head

The most obvious deviation from parallel structure appears in lists. Figure 5-5 shows a list that lacks parallel structure.

Deviation from parallel structure can also appear in text, as shown in Figure 5-6.

SECTION 5

OURSYSTEM STATEMENTS

OURSYSTEM statements establish program names, program characteristics, and operations to be performed at . . . .

SUBROUTINE CALLS

Subroutine calls transfer control to a subroutine and effect a return to the main logic path of the XYZ program . . . .

CALL Statement

The CALL statement unconditionally transfers control to the subroutine. The statement consists of the CALL . . . .

RETURN Statement

The RETURN statement provides the linkage back to the main path of the XYZ program. The statement consists . . . .

SORT OPERATIONS (SORT)

The SORT statement causes input records to be sorted in alphabetic order. You can designate an ascending or a descending sort sequence by including special parameters. The two types of SORT statements are described in the following paragraphs.

Ascending SORT Statement

The ascending SORT statement arranges information in ascending order according to the internal code of the . . . .

Descending SORT Statement

The descending SORT statement arranges information in descending order according to the internal code of the . . . .

FIGURE 5-4 Filled Section and Paragraph Head

Each word in the control header is defined as follows:

Word 1   a numeric code associated with the program
Word 2   the head/track location for storing the program
Word 3   the starting address for loading the program
Word 4   this word is set to 7777 if an error occurs during read mode

                                              ↑
                                              └──────── Not parallel

The explanation for Word 4 is not consistent with the explanations for Words 1, 2, and 3. The list is clear, but would have been parallel and would have reflected quality structure if Word 4 had read:

Word 4   a flag that is set to 7777 on read mode error

FIGURE 5-5 Writing Parallel Lists

Routines A, B, and C are utility routines that can be called by the EXECUTIVE program to perform specific functions. They are stored in the . . . .

Routine A handles the input processing for . . . .
. . . .

Routine B performs validity checks for . . . .
. . . .

Routine C is a process that associates hardware devices . . . .
. . . .

                                              ↑
                                              └──────── Not parallel

The lead-in text for Routine C is not consistent with the preceding paragraphs. The text is clear, but would have been parallel and would have reflected quality structure if the lead-in text for Routine C had read:

Routine C associates hardware devices . . . .

FIGURE 5-6 Writing Parallel Text

STRUCTURING TEXT

Structured text is information that can be seen at a glance. Here is a sentence with unstructured text:

> When a CHECKSUM clause is included in the WRITE statement, the appropriate routine is called before the data is moved into the output buffer, before conversion is attempted, and after standard system checks are completed.

Here is the same sentence with structured text:

> When a CHECKSUM clause is included in the WRITE statement, the appropriate routine is called as follows:
>   before the data is moved into the output buffer
>   before conversion is attempted
>   after standard system checks are completed.

Whenever you structure text, you are highlighting important issues, making information easier to retain, and increasing the usability of the manual. In other words, whenever you structure text, you are:

> highlighting important issues
> making information easier to retain
> increasing the usability of the manual.

6/ENSURING

READABILITY

What is readability?

Readability is the absence of jargon and slang.
Readability is never having to read twice.
Readability is consistent terminology.
Readability is short paragraphs.
Readability is short sentences.
Readability is continuity.
Readability is clarity.

Writing straightforward text about a complicated subject and writing it quickly requires talent, training, and experience. Even if you possess these qualifications, you could be clinging to old habits that undermine the quality of your writing.

This chapter offers simple guidelines that help to instill readability into software manuals.

FAVOR ACTIVE VOICE

Use active voice whenever possible. The words *whenever possible* are important words to remember. Not every sentence can be changed from passive to active voice. For example:

> The number of data blocks in an output file is computed by the TRANSFER program. (Passive voice)
>
> The TRANSFER program computes the number of data blocks in an output file. (Improved by the change to active voice)
>
> If the condition is satisfied, the SEARCH statement is executed. (This sentence cannot be changed to active voice. We do not know what will satisfy the condition or what portion of the software will trigger execution of the SEARCH statement.)

NEVER SAY MAY*

How many times have you seen a sentence like this in a software manual?

> You may initialize the equipment by pressing switch 1.

Did you know exactly what it was saying? If so, which of the following interpretations did you select?

1. You have the capability to initialize the equipment by pressing switch 1.
2. You have the manufacturer's permission to initialize the equipment by pressing switch 1.
3. It is possible that you are going to initialize the equipment by pressing switch 1.

*Material in this section has been adapted from C. Browning, "Technical Communication," *Journal of the Society for Technical Communication Correspondence,* 28, 3, Third Quarter 1981, 61-62.

If you selected sentence 1, you insulted the writer. According to *Webster's New Collegiate Dictionary,* the word *may* is archaic when used as a synonym for *can.* The word *may* appears in many documents associated with unchanging or legalistic disciplines. Wills, insurance policies, and government publications use the word *may* extensively, leaving the precise meaning to be interpreted by individuals or perhaps arbitration. Look at your IRS forms and instructions!

If you selected sentence 2, you implied that the writer insulted the customer. It is presumptuous for a writer to assume that a manufacturer can grant or deny permission to use equipment that sells for thousands, maybe millions of dollars. Customers will initialize the equipment by pressing switch 1 any time they please. For all the writer knows, customers will press switch 2 if they can get away with it.

If you selected sentence 3, you understood a grammatically correct sentence that conveyed absolutely no information.

The problem can be resolved by never using the word *may.*

Do you know exactly what the following sentence is saying?

You can initialize the equipment by pressing switch 1.

It would be difficult to provide more than one interpretation.

This brings up an interesting question: What should I do when I really want to infer possibility? What about this sentence?

An error may occur . . .

The sentence can be rewritten. For example:

Under certain circumstances an error occurs . . .
An error could occur . . .
An error might occur . . .

Programmers cannot afford to guess at the precise meaning of any word. The words *can* for capability and *might* for possibility guarantee readability. The word *may* guarantees ambiguity.

UNNECESSARY HYPHENATION IS OLD-FASHIONED

Hyphenation is spelled c-l-u-t-t-e-r. Software manuals with their sample programs have many special characters, and unnecessary hyphens only represent additional distraction for the reader.

Hyphens have been dying for years. Check the dictionary and you will find many single words that were hyphenated when you attended school. How often have you seen these words hyphenated?

> reentry   uppercase   lowercase   multiphase
> nonresident   reinsert   shutdown

The dictionary devotes an entire page to words that begin with the prefix *non* but do not use the hyphen. Whenever you are tempted to hyphenate a word, try checking the dictionary to see if it changed since you last used it.

Hyphens are real troublemakers in an automated text processing environment. Whenever you hyphenate unnecessarily, you are causing extra work for the typesetter. Machines and their operators have enough trouble handling hyphenation at the end of the line without having to contend with extraneous hyphens running through the text.

PRONOUNS ARE UNPOPULAR

Three types of pronouns enjoy very little status in software manuals. The indefinite pronoun is usually burdensome, sexist pronouns are always irritating, and the neuter pronoun has been known to destroy the meaning of a sentence.

The next three paragraphs discuss why these pronouns should either be eliminated from a software manual or at least used sparingly.

The Indefinite Pronoun

The indefinite pronoun *there* lengthens sentences and rarely adds readability. Sometimes the word is useful, but whenever possible, throw it away. For example:

> There are five I/O routines that can be called by Program A.

should be changed to read:

> Five I/O routines can be called by Program A.

and then be changed to active voice:

> Program A calls five I/O routines.

> The sentence has been reduced from 12 words to 6.

When you are looking for unnecessary hyphens, look for unnecessary indefinite pronouns.

Sexist Pronouns

The sexist pronouns *he, him, his, she,* and *her* are gradually disappearing from technical documentation. You have probably seen sentences like these:

1. After the operator has set appropriate flags, he can enter debug mode.
2. After the operator has set appropriate flags, he/she can enter debug mode.
3. After operators have set appropriate flags, they can enter debug mode.

Sentence 1 is annoying to some readers. Sentence 2 is cumbersome. Sentence 3 is implying multiple operators.

All sexist pronouns can be eliminated by exercising a little thought. Here are several alternatives.

After you have set appropriate flags, you can enter debug mode.

After setting appropriate flags, the operator can enter debug mode.

The operator must set appropriate flags before entering debug mode.

The neuter pronoun *it* is famous for chipping away at readability.

How many times have you read the word *it* and wondered what *it* really was? Look at this sentence:

The EXTEND directive alters execution of the SEARCH statement; it can appear anywhere within the job stream.

What can appear anywhere within the job stream? The EXTEND directive or the SEARCH statement?

How about this sentence?

After it updates the record, the REVISE routine unlocks the file.

If this sentence is read out of context, we cannot be sure who really updated the record. The pronoun *it* could be referring to the REVISE routine or to an antecedent in a preceding sentence. The reader would prefer redundancy to the vague pronoun *it*.

When you are looking for unnecessary indefinite pronouns, keep an eye out for neuter pronouns.

BYPASS PROGRAMMING JARGON

Programmers sometimes know their subjects too well. The result is jargon.

What is wrong with this sentence?

The new item is a group beginning with name-1 (if it is an elementary item) or the first elementary item in name-1 (if it is a group item).

Everything!

1. Two important thoughts are squeezed into one sentence.
2. The meaning of the sentence depends on the correct placement of the parenthetical phrases. (Parenthetical phrases in software manual text, by the way, detract from readability.)
3. The vague pronoun *it* adds to the confusion.

Here is the translation:

- If name-1 is an elementary item, the new item is a group that begins with name-1.
- If name-1 is a group item, the new item is a group that begins with the first elementary item in name-1.

You rarely get away with passing along programming jargon that creeps into specifications. Someone always manages to find it and ask you for an explanation.

QUOTATION MARKS CAN BE "DANGEROUS"

A terminal once issued this statement to an operator:

TYPE "EXIT"

The operator typed

"EXIT"

and received a terse error message that said:

QUOTATION MARKS ARE ILLEGAL

Quotation marks are common input characters in the computer industry. Programming language literals, for example, usually require quotation marks. Unless quotation marks are actual computer entry characters, they should never appear.

Some writers use quotation marks to indicate slang, which certainly does not belong in a professional technical document.

Some writers use quotation marks for emphasis. Emphasis can be handled by italics. If your production department does not have an italics font, you could approach staff members and remind them it is better to buy italics capability than to have customers wasting time trying to read around hordes of quotation marks. If staff members are not impressed, you can simply stop worrying about emphasis and restructure your sentences.

Any sentence can be rewritten to avoid quotation marks. These characters have no place in software manuals unless they represent valid input characters for a computer program.

THAT VERSUS WHICH

Remember the nonrestrictive clause? The nonrestrictive clause is not vital to the meaning of a sentence, is always introduced by the word *which,* and is always surrounded by commas. For example:

The I/O routine, *which is called by EXEC,* performs the processing.

Nonrestrictive clause—the commas are present.

This sentence implies that the program has only one I/O routine; the fact that the routine is called by EXEC is incidental.

Remember the restrictive clause? The restrictive clause is vital to the meaning of a sentence, can be introduced by the word *which,* and must not be surrounded by commas. For example:

The I/O routine *which is called by EXEC* performs the processing.

Restrictive clause—the commas are missing.

This sentence implies that the program has more than one I/O routine; the fact that this I/O routine is the one called by EXEC is critical.

The two sentences are entirely different.

The meaning of sentences should never have to depend on the presence or absence of commas. Commas can be inadvertently inserted or deleted during review, editing, and production. Commas have been known to drop out during printing.

To ensure readability, the word *which* should never be used in restrictive clauses. The word *that* should be used instead.

If the sentence with the restrictive clause had been written

The I/O routine *that is called by EXEC* performs the processing.

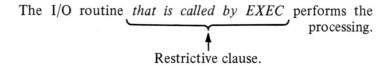

Restrictive clause.

everyone would have left it alone, and the meaning would have remained intact.

MAKING REFERENCES

Occasional references direct the reader to important additional information; extraneous references interrupt the reader's train of thought.

References are divided into four categories:

- in-section references
- out-of-section references
- out-of-manual references
- directional references

In-Section References

In-section references are rarely necessary. They usually appear because the text is improperly organized.

This is an in-section reference:

You can move the new records to the record buffer. The record buffer is described later in this section.

This in-section reference to the record buffer could be avoided in one of the following ways:

1. Provide an immediate definition of the record buffer and let the reader reach the description when it becomes appropriate.
2. Delay any mention of the record buffer until you are ready to provide the description.

Out-of-Section References

Out-of-section references are occasionally necessary, particularly in reference manuals. Sometimes, however, they appear because undefined terms are introduced.

This is an unnecessary out-of-section reference:

The program verifies the password and displays the screen selected by the operator. Refer to the main menu in Section 2.

Here the writer could not wait to send the reader away to look at the main menu. This out-of-section reference could be eliminated by the following sentence:

The program verifies the password and displays a main menu screen from which the operator makes selections.

Out-of-Manual References

Out-of-manual references are frequently necessary, but too many references to other manuals can be discouraging to the reader.

This is an out-of-manual reference:

You can conserve disk space by calling the PACK routine.

Refer to the System Reference Manual for a description of the PACK routine.

Out-of-manual references can be avoided when the information being referenced is not too long or too detailed. If the description of the PACK routine in the System Reference Manual is only a short paragraph, you can duplicate the text rather than reference the manual. When you repeat small blocks of text from other manuals, the reader does not have to keep looking elsewhere for needed information. But remember, information is always subject to change. If that duplicated block of text changes in the original manual, you have one more update to handle; this is a serious consideration if both manuals are not updated at the same time.

When making a decision, always weigh the alternatives.

Directional References

Directional references are not always what they seem to be.

This is a directional reference:

The I/O routine is described below.

This type of reference is always interesting when *below* turns out to be two pages downstream. What if the manual is printed in two columns? *Below* could be in the next column and really be *above.*

Here is another directional reference:

The I/O routine described above is called by the EXECU-TIVE program.

This type of reference has been known to send the reader around the corner and back one or more pages. Like the below direction in the two-column manual, *above* could end up being *below.*

When you are tempted to use a directional reference, think about how update material can move text. When you include a directional reference, consider what will happen if the update writer inserts five pages of text above or below your reference.

AVOID MULTIPLE PHRASES AND CLAUSES

Multiple phrases + multiple clauses = long sentences, and long sentences = poor readability.

This sentence has too many phrases and clauses:

When the PROC routine reads a record with a control field that does not contain an X, Y, or Z, or in which the control word does not indicate the expected file type, the routine returns an error 300 to the main program, which in turn displays the message text and aborts the job.

Sentences like this one can be divided into small segments for readability.

The PROC routine returns an error 300 to the main program under either of the following conditions:

1. The record control field does not contain an X, Y, or Z.
2. The control word does not indicate the expected file type.

The main program in turn displays the error 300 message and aborts the job.

BE CONSISTENT

What is wrong with these two sentences?

The TERMCOLUMNS field specifies the number of columns available on the terminal screen.

The TERMROWS field indicates the number of rows available on the terminal screen.

Nothing really, except *specifies* and *indicates* are synonyms in these two sentences. Synonyms are popular in creative writing, but they can cause confusion in software manuals. When synonyms are adjacent in text, as in the two sample sentences, readers will automatically pause and wonder if they should detect some shade of difference in the meaning. Readers prefer redundancy to synonyms.

Consistent terminology adds quality.

Does the program write records *on* disk or *to* disk?

Is *disk* spelled *disk* or *disc*?

Does the operator *press, hit, depress,* or even *strike* terminal keys?

Do programs *deliver, give, output,* or *display* error messages?

Consistent names eliminate confusion.

Is the TRANSFER program referred to as the Transfer program, the TRANSFER program, TRANSFER, or even XFER?

Consistent conventions add clarity.

Can the value be 1–100, 1 to 100, or 1 through 100?

REMEMBER YOUR FOREIGN READERS

Any software manual today is subject to international audiences. When you are writing in English, the international language, it is important to remember these readers.

They have several major complaints:

1. They dislike synonyms, whether or not they are adjacent. They must first determine if words really are synonyms and then translate accordingly. They wish writers would select a word and stay with it.
2. They are often mystified by American slang. They are not familiar with words like *cop-out* and *pretty good.*

3. They can be confused by Americanized examples that deal with unfamiliar subjects like Social Security numbers and baseball scores.

4. They don't (make that do not) like contractions. While you are trying to make your writing user-friendly, you might be alienating someone whose native language is not English.

WATCH OUT FOR STILTED TEXT

Readers, be they experts or beginners, desire software manuals that may be effectively utilized.

You have just read stilted text that was trying to say

Experts as well as beginners want software manuals that are easy to use.

Ensure readability.

7 / ARRANGING THE FRONT MATTER

Software technical writers eventually find themselves at the end of a hazardous writing trail only to be confronted by a menace called front matter. Some writers consider front matter boring work that should be sloughed off on an unsuspecting production editor. Most readers consider front matter important reference material. All technical publications managers expect to see it on the first review cycle.

Front matter generally consists of four types of material:

- revision record
- preface
- table of contents
- syntax conventions

Generating front matter is a fairly automatic process. However, these mundane items that comprise front matter do have an important effect on your software manuals, and this chapter explains why.

Software documentation is constantly changing, which is a good thing. If documentation for a specific product stops changing, it means research and development for that product has stopped. If all documentation suddenly becomes static, you can be sure the company has either designed perfect products to accommodate the next ten generations or is going bankrupt.

The revision record is a history of product development. This sheet of paper merely lists the publication of each revision and indicates what new features have been incorporated. Obviously, any organized publications department would keep records of this type, so why should it appear in the front matter?

Because it can never get lost as long as it is a permanent part of a printed manual.

All revision levels of software reference manuals and user manuals look a great deal alike on the outside. You can usually tell one revision level from another by looking in a corner of the cover to find a meaningless string of characters. CO692479B00, for example, could be one of these strings. Perhaps the CO stands for COBOL, 692479 an identifying number for the publication, and B00 the second revision. Not having time to decipher these codes, the reader goes directly to the revision record to see what is happening.

A typical revision record is shown in Figure 7-1. You will agree that it is more meaningful than CO692479B00. The reader who is using a system that is not upgraded to include the features listed for revision D will want to stay with revision C.

WRITING AN EFFECTIVE PREFACE

You have heard the comment, "Nobody ever reads the preface." And it is probably true. If nobody ever reads the preface, why should it appear in the front matter?

```
┌──────────────────────────────────────────────────────────────┐
│          REVISION RECORD FOR PUBLICATION 692479                │
│                                                                │
│   REVISION                      DESCRIPTION                    │
│                                                                │
│       A          Original manual for OURSYSTEM release level A01.│
│    08/12/82                                                    │
│                                                                │
│       B          This revision includes the RENEW Facility that enables the│
│    03/22/83      system operator to restore a partially damaged data base.│
│                  Release level B00.                            │
│                                                                │
│       C          This revision includes three new condition test statements:│
│    09/04/83      IF NOT, IF AND, IF OR. Release level C03.     │
│                                                                │
│       D          This revision includes the REWRITE Facility for the│
│    01/26/84      OURSYSTEM file handler. Release level D01.     │
│                                                                │
└──────────────────────────────────────────────────────────────┘
```

FIGURE 7-1 Sample Revision Record

Because it establishes the intent of the manual.

The preface identifies the audience. If, for example, you have written a user manual for a system analyst and pointed this out very carefully in the preface, you are protected against comments from customers who tried giving it to their data entry operators.

The preface aids the reader by supplying references to related and prerequisite material. This is especially important for reference manuals, which can never be completely self-contained. The preface also aids the writer. If, for example, you have written an application programming reference manual and listed the operating system manual as required reading, you have recourse against the programmer who does not believe in reading prefaces.

A sample preface is shown in Figure 7-2. Notice that the product is designed for data entry operators, but the manual is written for application programmers.

It is important to remember that prefaces cannot be completely standardized. No two are ever exactly alike.

PREFACE

This manual describes ULTIMATE as implemented for the OURSYSTEM Operating System.

ULTIMATE is an online report generator designed specifically for individuals inexperienced in the field of data processing. The ULTIMATE language consists of simple directives that allow data entry operators to access a corporation data base, select specific fields of information, and print formatted reports.

The manual is designed for programmers who are writing applications for the ULTIMATE product. Section 1 identifies the components that comprise the ULTIMATE product; Section 2 describes the ULTIMATE commands and associated options; and Section 3 describes the conventions established for compiler language interface.

Prerequisite material is contained in the following publication:

Introduction to ULTIMATE

Related material is contained in the following publications:

OURSYSTEM Operating System Reference Manual
OURSYSTEM Operating System User Manual

FIGURE 7-2 Sample Preface

ANALYZING THE TABLE OF CONTENTS

You have heard the comment, "Everybody reads the table of contents." And it is probably not true. Readers scan the table of contents once and then promptly forget it exists, turning to more important things like the index. Even if the table of contents is the least read part of your software manual, it is an important part of the front matter.

The table of contents is responsible for several things long before it reaches final form for printing:

- It assures the writer that all information is included.
- It assures the writer that information is properly organized; unbalanced paragraph heads show up very clearly.

- It assures production personnel that all information is accounted for and properly referenced.
- It indicates whether or not the manual has usability.

This last item might come as a surprise, but the table of contents is an indication of how good or how bad the software manual really is.

Figure 7-3 shows part of a poor table of contents. Read it and you will discover you have no idea what Section 7 is all about. Several things are wrong with it. Here are a few outstanding problems:

1. The section title *Directory* is meaningless.
2. The word *Overview* is trite.
3. The word *Considerations* is almost an industry standard for material that is left over and needs some place to go.

Figure 7-4 shows the same table of contents with more meaningful titles. Read it and you will discover you have some

FIGURE 7-3 Vague Table of Contents

CONTENTS

FIGURE 7-4 Clear Table of Contents

idea what Section 7 is all about. Notice that the *Considerations* entries are gone. Presumably a home was found for the information.

A table of contents usually proclaims the usability of the software manual. Maybe nobody will read it, but it is a bellwether for the pages that follow.

ESTABLISHING SYNTAX CONVENTIONS

Syntax is the orderly arrangement of language elements.
English syntax looks like this:

If your checkbook balance is less than $100, deposit money in the bank; otherwise, go shopping.

The same sentence in programming language syntax might look something like this:

IF bank-book-balance(n) [IS] $\left\{\begin{matrix} \text{LESS THAN} \\ < \end{matrix}\right\}$ integer

PERFORM routine-1
ELSE PERFORM routine-2.

The brackets, braces, uppercase letters, lowercase letters, and punctuation in programming language syntax are meaningful.

When these conventions are used throughout a manual, they need to be explained only once. They appear in the front matter and are usually positioned immediately after the table of contents.

A sample syntax conventions page is shown in Figure 7-5.

SYNTAX CONVENTIONS

Syntax is presented throughout the manual to illustrate elements used in the ULTIMATE language. The following list summarizes the characters and symbols used in the syntax notation.

UPPERCASE LETTERS   Uppercase letters are preassigned keywords and must be entered exactly as shown.

lowercase letters   Lowercase letters represent variable items to be supplied by the programmer; the words shown indicate the characteristics of the information they represent.

Brackets [　]   Brackets enclose optional elements that can be included or omitted.

Braces {　}   Braces enclose required elements; only one element can be selected.

Punctuation   Punctuation characters are essential where shown and must be included; other punctuation characters can be used as specified in the manual.

FIGURE 7-5 Sample Syntax Conventions Page

8/PREPARING

THE

BACK MATTER

The term *back matter* could be a misnomer when applied to software manuals. In ordinary books, back matter is supplementary reference material that is casually ignored by most readers. In software manuals, back matter is a collection of dog-eared pages with penciled notations, coffee stains, and fingerprints.

Back matter in both reference manuals and user manuals generally consists of three types of material:

- appendixes
- glossary
- index

Generating back matter is a very time-consuming process, but mechanics exist and can be applied in this very important area.

Software manual back matter usually includes a number of appendixes. Error messages, for example, almost always appear in back matter. What is important information like error messages doing in a place like this? Error messages, like several other types of material, belong to a category that is more suitable to an appendix than to the main text.

Information that is usually relegated to an appendix falls into one of two categories:

1. Information that encompasses the entire product, such as:
   error messages
   character sets
   character conversion tables
   mathematics tables
   reserved words
   language syntax summaries
   data entry procedure summaries
2. Information that is highly specialized, directed toward a small percentage of readers, or used infrequently, such as:
   system recovery procedures
   file conversion
   peripheral device selection
   version upward/downward compatibility
   configuration guidelines

The two most common appendixes are error messages and summaries of programming language syntax or data entry procedures. The following paragraphs discuss efficient ways to prepare them.

Including Error Messages

The only thing worse than getting an error in your program is discovering the manual neglected to tell you what to do about it.

Error messages are frequently numbered and maintained in diagnostic libraries, in which case you can get a listing of these libraries to verify the wording of the messages. If error messages are not maintained in diagnostic libraries, you must rely on the programmer to supply them. This, of course, is the easy part. Now you have to provide the explanations.

Providing adequate explanations for error messages requires a familiarity with the internal software. Even if you had time in your writing schedule to trace the course of error messages through program listings, you could not do a thorough job.

The shortest route to adequate explanations is a straight line to the responsible programmer. Having the programmer write down all but the obvious explanations produces the following results:

- Explanations are sufficiently detailed.
- Explanations are correct.
- Your time is saved.
- The programmer's time is saved; extensive review will not be necessary.
- The reader's biggest problem is resolved.

Error messages must be arranged so that readers can find them as quickly as possible. Readers are not interested in reading the message itself because they are already looking at it on their terminal screen or program listing. They are interested in the explanation so they can make corrections and get on with their work.

You can position error messages in tables to help readers find the explanations quickly. Be sure to put

numbered error messages in numeric order

and

unnumbered error messages in alphabetic order.

An example of a partial error message appendix is shown in Figure 8-1.

APPENDIX A

OURCOMPILER ERROR MESSAGES

Error messages relating to source statements are divided into two categories: fatal and warning, indicated by the error code F or W.

A fatal error inhibits execution of the OURCOMPILER compiler. A maximum of 40 fatal errors can be recorded; when this number is exceeded, compilation terminates.

A warning error does not inhibit execution, but indicates a deviation from the usual coding; errors could occur at execute time. A maximum of 40 warning errors can be recorded; when this number is exceeded, compilation continues and warning messages are suppressed.

Error messages appear in sentence form and immediately follow the statement in error on the source program listing. When one or more fatal errors are encountered, the message COMPILATION UNSUCCESSFUL is displayed on the terminal at the end of compilation and on printer output when applicable.

Compiler error messages are listed in Table A-1. The Error Code column indicates whether the message is fatal (F) or warning (W).

Table A-1. Compiler Error Messages

Error Number	Error Code	Message	Definition
200	F	TABLE TOO LARGE	The directory table exceeds 480 bytes. Increase the extent of the table or reduce the number of entries.
201	F	INVALID STATEMENT NUMBER	The statement number is not within the 1 through 86408 range.

──────►

FIGURE 8-1 Sample Error Message Appendix

Error Number	Error Code	Message	Definition
202	W	MISSING END STATEMENT	The compiler encountered source input limit but did not encounter an END statement. An END statement has been inserted and the program has terminated normally.
203	F	INVALID OPERAND COMBINATION	An operation was attempted on operands that were not both decimal or both binary. Change the description of one operand in the Describe Section of the program.
204	W	UNEQUAL OPERAND LENGTHS	The lengths of the operands are unequal and this could result in truncation of low-order digits. To avoid truncation, increase the size of the result field.
205	F	TOO MANY TABLES	More than 50 tables have been defined.
206	F	STATEMENT NUMBER ON TABLE	A statement number appeared on a table definition statement. Table definition statements must not have statement numbers.

FIGURE 8-1 (cont.)

Programming languages and operating systems always have syntax. This syntax, which is scattered throughout the manual, must be summarized in an appendix for quick reference. Readers might remember most statements or instructions, but they cannot be expected to memorize long lists of parameters.

The organization of the product determines how syntax should be summarized.

- Syntax for languages that have natural divisions would be summarized within the divisions and would be summarized alphabetically or by position, depending on the product. Organizing by division reminds the reader that program order is just as important as correct syntax. The COBOL language is a typical example of a language with divisions.
- Languages that do not have natural divisions would be summarized alphabetically or by position, depending on the product.

Figure 8-2 shows a partial sample syntax summary for a language that has divisions. Figure 8-3 shows a partial sample syntax summary for a language that does not have divisions.

Notice that these two illustrations include page numbers. Page numbers represent a small amount of extra work for you but a lot of help for the reader. When you include page numbers, make sure the numbers reference to the *beginning* of explanatory text for the syntax, not merely to the same illustrated syntax.

Summarizing Data Entry Procedures

Data entry systems frequently have syntax that is similar to, but certainly not as complicated as, the syntax in programming languages and operating systems. Software manuals that describe data entry systems need procedure summaries for instant reference.

Figure 8-4 shows a partial procedure summary for a data entry system. This summary is not quite the same as the syntax summaries for a programming language. Application program-

APPENDIX B

OURCOMPILER SYNTAX SUMMARY

OURCOMPILER syntax is summarized in this appendix. Detailed information for each command is referenced by page number.

FIGURE 8-2 Sample Syntax Summary for Language with Divisions

APPENDIX C

OURCOMPILER SYNTAX SUMMARY

OURCOMPILER syntax is summarized in this appendix. Detailed information for each command is referenced by page number.

Page

ADD $\begin{Bmatrix} \text{data-name} \\ \text{constant} \end{Bmatrix}$ TO $\begin{Bmatrix} \text{data-name} \\ \text{constant} \end{Bmatrix}$.   4-4

CALL statement-number .   4-6

DIVIDE $\begin{Bmatrix} \text{data-name} \\ \text{constant} \end{Bmatrix}$ INTO $\begin{Bmatrix} \text{data-name} \\ \text{constant} \end{Bmatrix}$.   4-7

END   4-8

MOVE $\begin{Bmatrix} \text{data-name} \\ \text{constant} \end{Bmatrix}$ TO $\begin{Bmatrix} \text{data-name} \\ \text{constant} \end{Bmatrix}$.   4-9

MULTIPLY $\begin{Bmatrix} \text{data-name} \\ \text{constant} \end{Bmatrix}$ BY $\begin{Bmatrix} \text{data-name} \\ \text{constant} \end{Bmatrix}$.   4-11

SUBTRACT $\begin{Bmatrix} \text{data-name} \\ \text{constant} \end{Bmatrix}$ FROM $\begin{Bmatrix} \text{data-name} \\ \text{constant} \end{Bmatrix}$.   4-13

TABLE table-name $\begin{Bmatrix} \text{N} \\ \text{A} \end{Bmatrix}$ constant [, constant . . .] .   4-15

FIGURE 8-3 Sample Syntax Summary for Language without Divisions

mers need detailed information in these summaries. They will be referencing your manual when they develop additional procedures for the product.

Sometimes data entry systems need other types of information centralized in an appendix. A typical example is information related to system operation. Figure 8-5 shows a partial operating procedure summary for a data entry system.

APPENDIX D

ˈSUMMARY OF OURREPORTER DIRECTIVES

OURREPORTER directive formats are summarized in this appendix. Detailed information for each format is referenced by page number.

Page

DELETE record-name	Delete a record from the data base.	3-2
DISPLAY field-name [field-name] . . .	Display all data base information stored in one or more fields.	3-6
END	End the OURREPORTER procedure.	3-7
HELP message-number	Ask for the explanation of an error message number.	3-9
INSERT record-name	Insert a new record in the data base.	3-10
PREPARE report-name FROM report-file-name	Prepare a report.	3-12
REWIND file-name	Rewind a file to the beginning of information.	3-15
TITLE IS title [CENTERED]	Supply a report title with an option to have it centered on the page.	3-16

FIGURE 8-4 Sample Summary for Data Entry Procedures

ESTABLISHING A GLOSSARY

A glossary is to an analyst and a programmer what a dictionary is to a writer. No one can be expected to remember all the words and their meanings all the time. Analysts and program-

APPENDIX E

SUMMARY OF OURSYSTEM OPERATIONS

OURREPORTER directives can only be issued after some dialog exchange takes place between you and the OURSYSTEM Operating System. Follow the steps in the order shown.

Type LOGON your-name, password	The system signs on and prints ENTER COMMAND
Type OURREPORTER	The system prints
	OURREPORTER IS READY ?
Enter OURREPORTER directives	
Type END	The system prints
	OURREPORTER SIGNING OFF ENTER COMMAND
Type LOGOUT	The system signs off.

FIGURE 8-5 Sample Summary for Data Entry Operations

mers have the additional task of contending with myriad acronyms and mnemonics.

A glossary is an important part of a software manual, even when terms are carefully defined the first time they appear. For example:

An excellent definition of a term in Section 2 is of little value to the reader who is reading out of context and discovers the term for the first time in Section 17.

An excellent definition of a term in Section 2 is of little value to the reader who is reading in context but reaches Section 17 and forgets the definition along with the Section 2 page number where it appeared.

Readers need glossaries. They need them whether they are reading in or out of context.

Developing organizations also need glossaries. They need them to help maintain consistency among products. If glossary terms are not standardized, organizations could end up with interfacing software products that carry entirely different meanings for the same term.

Remember to include acronyms and mnemonics. If the product is named A GENeral Translator but is called AGENT, be sure to include both entries. If the product has a TRANS-FER program that is named XFER in the program call, include them both also.

Terms should be defined the first time they appear in a software manual. If you define each term twice, once in your draft and once on another piece of paper, you will not have to prepare a glossary. It will be finished whenever you are.

INDEXING

A software manual without an index is comparable to a library without a catalog system. Everything is there, but just try to find it!

Because software reference manuals concentrate on making information easy to locate, the index is a natural adjunct. No matter how carefully you have organized the manual, you still need the index.

Because software user manuals concentrate on presenting information in logical order, the index is the key to locating particular subjects.

Readers will put up with just about anything but a bad index. Give them an index that is nothing more than an inverted table of contents and they will probably write to your organization and complain. Leave out the index and they will insist they received a manual with pages missing.

Knowing how readers feel about indexes, you can go one step further and create what is frequently called an instant index. This is sure to increase the popularity of your manual. If you are convinced that one index is all you can handle, read on and discover how easily you can generate both types of indexes.

Great strides are being made toward the development of completely automated index generators. Many organizations in the meantime have developed programs that automate the entry, positioning, and permutation of index items.

This is good news, but the fact remains that almost all writers still must decide exactly what items go into an index.

And this is even better news. A simple procedure can be used to prepare a standard index, and it involves only a few steps.

1. Make a complete copy of the manual.
2. Starting on page 1, highlight each important word or phrase with a highlighter pen.
3. When you have finished highlighting the last page, return to page 1 and begin making entries, organizing them into main and subordinate entries as appropriate. For example, you would make the term *ADD statement* a main entry under the A listings, the word *Statement* a main entry under the S listings, and the word *ADD* a subordinate entry under the word *Statement.* Be sure to include not only words that actually appear in the text but also other related words or synonyms that might be significant to your readers.

Figure 8-6 illustrates this procedure. The left-hand page of the illustration shows a sample page of text with appropriate words and phrases highlighted. The right-hand page shows the building of the standard index for that page. You probably would never have this many entries for a single page, and if you did, you would be merging or dropping many of the items in the final pass.

Just like the table of contents, the standard index reflects the usability of the manual. By glancing through the finished index, you can determine the organization of the manual. Indexes with entries that reference more than four or five page numbers indicate one of two things:

1. The organization of the manual is poor. If a specific index entry references too many page numbers and the numbers

SIGNAL CONTROL

Signal control is the setting of program and system flags to indicate the occurrence or nonoccurrence of predefined conditions. Control is performed by the SET statement, which can reference record signals and system signals.

Record Signals

Signals identified by numbers 1 through 37 are reserved for programmer use and are referred to as record signals. These signals serve as program flags for interrecord processing. After a record is processed and stored on disk, the record is no longer available for testing or referencing. Relevant information can be preserved from one record to another through the record signals.

The syntax for setting record signals is:

```
SET  RECSIGNAL  { n   }
                { n-n }
```

where n is an integer from 1 through 37.

System Signals

Signals identified by numbers 40 through 60 are referred to as system signals. These signals are set by the program when execution errors occur. System signals can be tested under program control.

The syntax for setting system signals is:

```
SET  SYSSIGNAL  { n   }
                { n-n }
```

where n is an integer from 40 through 60.

SUBROUTINE CALLS

Subroutine calls enable the programmer to transfer control to a subroutine to perform additional processing. Subroutine calls are performed by the CALL and RETURN statements.

The CALL statement unconditionally transfers control to the subroutine. The RETURN statement provides linkage back to the main program.

FIGURE 8-6 Creating a Standard Index

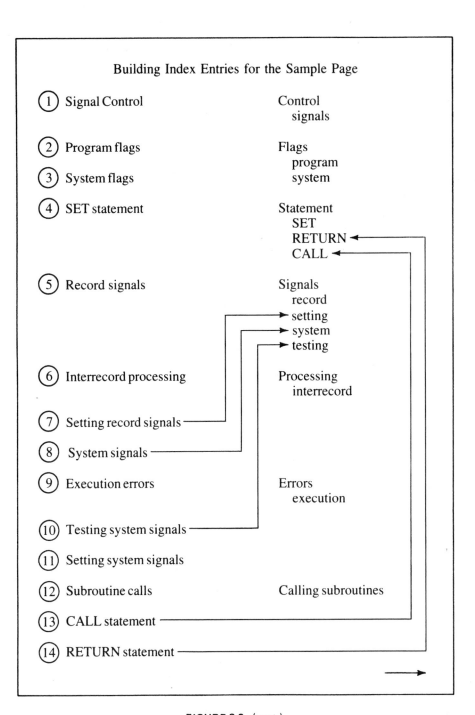

FIGURE 8-6 (cont.)

Alphabetizing the Index Entries

CALL statement
Calling subroutines
Control
   signals
Errors
   execution
Execution errors
Flags
   program
   system
Interrecord processing
Processing
   interrecord
Program flags
Record signals
RETURN statement
SET statement
Setting record signals
Setting system signals
Signal control
Signals
   record
   setting
   system
   testing
Statement
   CALL
   RETURN
   SET
Subroutine calls
System flags
System signals
Testing system signals

FIGURE 8-6 (cont.)

reflect various sections of the manual, information is scattered.

2. The index itself is poor. You have made one or both of the following mistakes:

You have included subsequent page numbers. If information for an item begins on page 4, for example, and continues onto page 5, only page 4 needs to be referenced. The one important exception to this rule occurs when you want to force the reader to page 5 because some critical piece of information is there and should not be overlooked.

You have found a common term, like *procedure* or *compilation,* that runs throughout the manual and you chose to reference it every time it appeared in the text.

Preparing an Instant Index

Back in Chapter 3 we discussed logical groupings called catalogs. Very large programming languages, like PL/I for example, frequently have extensive catalogs. Even though these catalogs become entry items in the standard index, they can be duplicated in another part of the manual to make life easier for the reader.

Where would they go? In the most convenient spot, which would be inside the back cover. If you needed more room, you could put some inside the front cover. Figure 8-7 shows a sample instant index.

STATEMENTS

ADD	6-3	IF	6-10	TABLE	6-26
CALL	6-5	MOVE	6-14	USE	6-30
DIVIDE	6-7	MULTIPLY	6-20	VERIFY	6-32
END	6-9	READ	6-22	WRITE	6-40

ATTRIBUTES

BINARY	3-2	EXT	3-7	INT	3-14
CHAR	3-3	FIXED	3-9	PIC	3-17
DECIMAL	3-5	FLOATING	3-12	REAL	3-27

FIGURE 8-7 Creating an Instant Index

9/PASSING

THE TEST

A software manual can appear to be a well-written and completely accurate document, yet fail the test of usability.

The following write-up organized in reference-text format represents this type of software manual. The text ignores many of the guidelines discussed in this book and, as a result, fails to meet the goal of a software manual. See if you can find 22 errors for a perfect score.

Errors and the line numbers on which they appeared follow the sample text.

An improved write-up follows the error explanations.

SECTION 9/

FILE

MANAGEMENT

File management is handled by the File Executive routine   1
that communicates with the operating system. It performs   2
several functions that usually are under program control: 3
transmits data to and from storage, controls equipment   4
assignment, maintains file security, and performs error   5
recovery.   6
    The capabilities of File Executive are available to the   7
user through the declaration of file structures and use of   8
system macros. By selecting appropriate file structures,   9
you can maximize utilization of processing time. By using   10
system macros, you can access the operating system in-   11
structions which are called from the main program. System   12
macros are described in Section 10.   13
     14
     15
     16
FILE TYPES   17
     18
     19
You may declare file type by entering the appropriate   19
value in the FILE parameter of the STRUCTURE state-   20
ment. The STRUCTURE statement is always the first   21

statement in the program. STRUCTURE statement syntax is:

STRUCTURE, FILE=file-type

There are three file types. Each type is described below.

Basic Files (BA)

You declare basic files by entering the characters BA as a FILE parameter. For example:

STRUCTURE, FILE=BA

Basic files do not have a formal structure. Data in this type of file is referenced by standard internal addressing methods rather than by logical record position. After basic files are created, they can be accessed only by File Executive. They can't be manipulated by the program.

Sequential Record Files (SR)

You declare sequential record files by entering the characters SR as a FILE parameter. For example:

STRUCTURE, FILE=SR

Sequential record files have a logical record structure. Logical record structure is a structure in which each record within the file has a logical predecessor and successor. A record is referenced by this logical record position.

File Executive calculates logical record position and passes this information to the program during processing. The operating system may add special control information when storing a record that is removed when the record is transmitted.

Structured Subfiles (SS)

You declare structured subfiles by entering the characters SS as a FILE parameter. For example:

Structured subfiles are files that hold temporary information; information in these subfiles can be passed back to sequential record files. Subfiles are frequently used to hold intermediate results during arithmetic processing.

You can define any number of subfiles in your program, but you must not access more than 10 subfiles simultaneously. If you attempt to access more than 10 subfiles at any one time, program data in the most recently accessed subfile will be undefined.

Structured subfile storage. File Executive assigns and controls storage for a subfile. When processing on a subfile terminates, the space occupied by the subfile becomes available to other subfiles. This convention provides an efficient operating environment.

FILE IDENTIFICATION

Files are identified to File Executive by system IDs. Three system IDs are used:

- PHYSID—physical ID
- LBLID—label ID
- INTID—internal ID

PHYSID (Physical ID)

PHYSID is assigned by the computer operator as he initializes the devices. The ID is a 28-character identifier that begins with a letter followed by 6 digits. This ID appears in all messages issued by the operator.

LBLID (Label ID)

LBLID is assigned by the program when a tape file is labeled. The ID is an 80-character identifier that consists of the file name, user name, and program name. Each

69
70
71
72
73
74
75
76
77
78
79
80
81
82
83
84
85
86
87
88
89
90
91
92
93
94
95
96
97
98
99
100
101
102
103
104
105
106
107
108
109
110
111

name is required and each is limited to 8 alphanumeric characters. Optional documentary text can follow the program name. This text is limited to 56 characters and can consist of "boilerplate" information that is copied from a user library.

INTID (Internal ID)

INTID is assigned by File Executive. The ID is a 6-character identifier that provides the means for the operating system to identify individual program requests, and during error recovery, assuming error recovery has been specified on your program RUN control command, provides the means to trace program activity.

FILE ALLOCATION

The total space dedicated to resident and non-resident files is determined at run time. File allocation can be dynamic, fixed, or segmented.

- *Dynamic Allocation.* Dynamic allocation is allocation of space in increments as required to perform read and write requests during program execution. The maximum amount of space that can be allocated at a given time is declared by an installation parameter.

- *Fixed Allocation.* Fixed allocation is allocation of space in a fixed number of words for program execution. Fixed allocation is declared by the ALLOC parameter of your program RUN control command. A fixed allocation of at least ALLOC = 74 is recommended.

- *Segmented Allocation.* Segmented allocation consists of a fixed number of contiguous blocks for program execution. Segmented allocation is declared by the SEG parameter of your program RUN command. Segmented allocation is recommended for structured subfiles. A segmented allocation of SEG = 2 is usually sufficient for one subfile.

Line 2

It performs several functions that usually are under program control.

The closest antecedent to the pronoun *it* is *operating system.* The section is discussing file management, which is handled by File Executive; therefore, *it* must refer to File Executive. The text is not clear and concise.

Line 3

. . . program control: transmits data to and from storage . . .

This is the beginning of a list that should be structured for emphasis and easy viewing by the reader. The four items following the colon should be listed, indented, and possibly preceded by bullets.

Line 7

The capabilities of File Executive are available to the user . . .

This sentence is not straightforward. Unlike the two sentences that immediately follow, the text appears in passive voice and refers to a *user* rather than *you,* the reader.

Line 10

. . . maximize utilization of processing time.

This is stilted text.

Line 11

. . . you can access the operating system instructions which are called from the main program.

The phrase *which are called* is restrictive and depends on the absence of the comma. The word *that* rather than *which* should have been used.

Line 19

You may declare file type by entering the appropriate . . .

The word *may* could be interpreted as possibility or permission. The text is subject to two interpretations, neither of which is correct; the writer really meant capability. The word *can* should have been used.

Line 27

There are three file types.

The indefinite pronoun *there* interferes with readability. Indefinite pronouns should be avoided.

Line 27

Each type is described below.

The word *below* is a directional reference. Directional references should never be used. If update material is added, the information *below* could be far away.

Line 39

. . . referenced by standard internal addressing methods rather than by logical record position.

Logical record position is an undefined term. Terms should be introduced and defined before they are referenced. Since the term is not even appropriate here, it should not have appeared.

Line 42

They can't be manipulated by the program.

Software manuals are subject to international audiences. Foreign readers dislike contractions. The word *can't* should have appeared as *cannot*.

Line 58

The operating system may add special control information . . .

Here is the word *may* again. This time the writer apparently meant possibility and should have avoided ambiguity by using the word *might*.

Line 59

. . . when storing a record that is removed when the record is transmitted.

The function word *that* is introducing a subordinate clause that appears to be referring to *record* but is actually referring to *control information*. The clause is misplaced, and the sentence is grammatically incorrect.

Line 76

If you attempt to access more than 10 subfiles at any one time, program data in the most recently accessed subfile will be undefined.

If you caught this, add 5 points to your score. Software manual text should be structured for emphasis, particularly when the text is pointing out that data can be destroyed. The sentence not only should have been indented for emphasis, it should have been preceded by a warning!

Line 80

Structured Subfile Storage

Here is an unbalanced paragraph head. The head was not even needed and should not have appeared.

Line 90

Three system IDs are used:

The system IDs are members of a named catalog. The listed system IDs and the subsequent paragraph heads describing them should have been alphabetized by system ID name.

Line 101

PHYSID is assigned by the computer operator as he initializes the devices.

Here is the sexist pronoun *he.* This is the most difficult type of correction you will ever have to make in software technical writing. The sample improved version at the end of this chapter offers one solution—perhaps you can find another.

Line 115

. . . can consist of "boilerplate" information that is copied from a user library.

Quotation marks should never appear unless they are actual computer entry characters. Here the writer was trying to indicate a coined word. Even if an italics font had been available, the word *boilerplate* borders on slang and is rarely necessary.

Line 121

The ID is a 6-character identifier that provides the means for the operating system to . . .

This long sentence with its multiple phrases and clauses completely loses the reader. The sentence lacks readability and should be rewritten.

Line 132

. . . resident and non-resident files . . .

Unnecessary hyphens add clutter to software manuals and increase the workload of the production staff. The word *nonresident,* like most words using the prefix *non,* is not a hyphenated word.

Line 140

The maximum amount of space that can be allocated at a given time is declared by an installation parameter.

Dropping hints about anything so important as an installation parameter is unfair. The reader who needs to know about this parameter deserves some kind of explanation. The text is not precise.

Line 150

Segmented allocation consists of a fixed number of contiguous blocks for program execution.

The text for this third member of the bulleted list is not parallel. The sentence should have read:

Segmented allocation is allocation of space in a fixed number of contiguous blocks for program execution.

Line 152

Segmented allocation is declared by the SEG parameter of your program RUN command.

You might have missed this one, but not very many readers would. The program RUN command was called program RUN control command in every other instance. Terminology should always be consistent.

The following write-up is an improved version of the *File Management* write-up that appeared at the beginning of this chapter. This text corrects the errors in the previous version by following the guidelines for effective software technical writing.

SECTION 9/

FILE

MANAGEMENT

IMPROVED

File management is handled by the File Executive routine that communicates with the operating system. File Executive performs several functions that usually are under program control:

- transmits data to and from storage
- controls equipment assignment
- maintains file security
- performs error recovery

You can take advantage of these File Executive capabilities by declaring file structures and using system macros. By selecting appropriate file structures, you can reduce processing time. By using system macros, you can access the operating system instructions that are called from the main program. System macros are described in Section 10.

FILE TYPES

You can declare file type by entering the appropriate value in the FILE parameter of the STRUCTURE statement. The STRUCTURE statement is always the first statement in the program. STRUCTURE statement syntax is:

STRUCTURE, FILE=file-type

Three file types are available:

- basic
- sequential record
- structured subfiles

Basic Files (BA)

You declare basic files by entering the characters BA as a FILE parameter. For example:

STRUCTURE, FILE=BA

Basic files do not have a formal structure. Data in this type of file is referenced by standard internal addressing methods. After basic files are created, they can be accessed only by File Executive. They cannot be manipulated by the program.

Sequential Record Files (SR)

You declare sequential record files by entering the characters SR as a FILE parameter. For example:

STRUCTURE, FILE=SR

Sequential record files have a logical record structure. Logical record structure is a structure in which each record within the file has a logical predecessor and successor. A record is referenced by this logical record position.

File Executive calculates logical record position and passes this information to the program during processing.

The operating system might add special control information to a record when the record is stored; this information is removed when the record is transmitted.

Structured Subfiles (SS)

You declare structured subfiles by entering the characters SS as a FILE parameter. For example:

STRUCTURE, FILE=SS

Structured subfiles are files that hold temporary information; information in these subfiles can be passed back to sequential record files. Subfiles are frequently used to hold intermediate results during arithmetic processing.

You can define any number of subfiles in your program, but you must not access more than 10 subfiles simultaneously.

WARNING: If you attempt to access more than 10 subfiles at any one time, program data in the most recently accessed subfile will be undefined.

File Executive assigns and controls storage for a subfile. When processing on a subfile terminates, the space occupied by the subfile becomes available to other subfiles. This convention provides an efficient operating environment.

FILE IDENTIFICATION

Files are identified to File Executive by system IDs. Three system IDs are used:

- INTID—internal ID
- LBLID—label ID
- PHYSID—physical ID

INTID (Internal ID)

INTID is assigned by File Executive. The ID is a 6-character identifier that allows the operating system to:

- identify individual program requests
- trace program activity when error recovery is specified on your program RUN control command.

LBLID (Label ID)

LBLID is assigned by the program when a tape file is labeled. The ID is an 80-character identifier that consists of the file name, user name, and program name. Each name is required and each is limited to 8 alphanumeric characters. Optional documentary text can follow the program name. This text is limited to 56 characters and can consist of standard information that is copied from a user library.

PHYSID (Physical ID)

PHYSID is assigned by the computer operator at device initialize time. The ID is a 28-character identifier that begins with a letter followed by 6 digits. This ID appears in all messages issued by the operator.

FILE ALLOCATION

The total space dedicated to resident and nonresident files is determined at run time. File allocation can be dynamic, fixed, or segmented.

- *Dynamic Allocation.* Dynamic allocation is allocation of space in increments as required to perform read and write requests during program execution. The maximum amount of space that can be allocated at a given time is declared by the OPTIONS installation parameter; the setting of this parameter is determined by the data administrator.
- *Fixed Allocation.* Fixed allocation is allocation of space in a fixed number of words for program execution. Fixed allocation is declared by the ALLOC parameter of your program RUN control command.

A fixed allocation of at least ALLOC = 74 is recommended.

- *Segmented Allocation.* Segmented allocation is allocation of space in a fixed number of contiguous blocks for program execution. Segmented allocation is declared by the SEG parameter of your program RUN control command. Segmented allocation is recommended for structured subfiles. A segmented allocation of SEG = 2 is usually sufficient for one subfile.

GLOSSARY

This glossary lists terms that appeared in the text. The definitions for these terms apply only to the manner in which the terms were used in this book.

ABBREVIATED CALLOUT   A callout that appears as a stand-alone or parenthesized phrase.

BACK MATTER   Material that appears in the back of a manual; usually consists of appendixes, glossary, and standard index.

BALANCED PARAGRAPH HEADS   At least two paragraph heads appearing on the same topic level.

CALLOUT   A reference to a numbered illustration or table.

CATALOG   A series of logical groupings.

CROSS-REFERENCE   A reference to another part of the same manual or to another manual.

DATA ENTRY PROCEDURE SUMMARY   A centralized listing of all data entry procedures that appear throughout a manual.

DIRECTIONAL REFERENCE A reference to information that is positioned above or below text.

EMPTY PARAGRAPH HEAD A paragraph head immediately followed by another paragraph head with no intervening text.

EMPTY SECTION HEAD A section head immediately followed by a paragraph head with no intervening text.

EXTERNAL SPECIFICATION See *Specification.*

FEATURE A capability of a software product.

FRONT MATTER Material that appears in the front of a manual; usually consists of a revision record, preface, table of contents, and syntax conventions.

IN-SECTION REFERENCE A reference to another part of the same section.

INSTANT INDEX An abbreviated index of common entities that appear throughout a manual.

NAMED CATALOG A series of logical groupings in which each member of the group has a specific name.

NONRESTRICTIVE CLAUSE A clause that is not vital to the meaning of a sentence.

OUT-OF-MANUAL REFERENCE A reference to another manual.

OUT-OF-SECTION REFERENCE A reference to another section of the same manual.

PARAGRAPH HEAD An identifying title for subsequent text.

PARALLEL TEXT Text that is consistent in style and in construction.

PREFACE Information that identifies the subject matter and audience of a manual.

RELEASE DATE The date on which an organization plans to deliver software to its customers.

RESTRICTIVE CLAUSE A clause that is vital to the meaning of a sentence.

REVISION RECORD A history of the development of and supporting documentation for a software product.

RUNNING HEAD An identifying line of information that appears on each page of a section, usually beginning on the second page.

SECTION HEAD An identifying title for a section of a manual.

SENTENCE CALLOUT A callout that appears as a complete sentence.

SHADING A technique in which specific information appears shaded to differentiate between what is entered by an individual and what is supplied by the computer system.

SOFTWARE REFERENCE MANUAL A complete description of a software product.

SOFTWARE TECHNICAL WRITER A technical writer who specializes in writing about computer software.

SOFTWARE USER MANUAL A manual that explains how to use a software product.

SPECIAL CHARACTERS Characters other than digits or letters.

SPECIFICATION A description of a software product written by a high-level analyst, stating objectives for the programming staff.

STANDARD INDEX The standard alphabetized listing of subjects and their page numbers in a software manual.

STRUCTURED TEXT Text that is arranged for emphasis and easy reading.

SYNTAX CONVENTIONS A centralized listing that explains how programming syntax is represented in a manual.

SYNTAX SUMMARY A centralized listing of all syntax that appears throughout a manual.

UNBALANCED PARAGRAPH HEAD A single paragraph head appearing on a topic level.

UPDATE MATERIAL New information or changes to existing information in a software manual.

INDEX

QA76.9.D6 B76 1984   c.1
Browning, Christine.   100107 000
Guide to effective software

3 9310 00054783 4
GOSHEN COLLEGE-GOOD LIBRARY